Living Simply Abundant

RECONCILING ABUNDANCE CONSCIOUSNESS
WITH LIFE ON A SMALL PLANET

R.FRANK ROBINSON

BALBOA.
PRESS

A DIVISION OF HAY HOUSE

Balboa Press books may be ordered through booksellers or by contacting:

Balboa Press
A Division of Hay House
1663 Liberty Drive
Bloomington, IN 47403
www.balboapress.com
1 (877) 407-4847

Because of the dynamic nature of the Internet, any web addresses or
links contained in this book may have changed since publication and
may no longer be valid. The views expressed in this work are solely those
of the author and do not necessarily reflect the views of the publisher,
and the publisher hereby disclaims any responsibility for them.

The author of this book does not dispense medical advice or prescribe the use
of any technique as a form of treatment for physical, emotional, or medical
problems without the advice of a physician, either directly or indirectly. The
intent of the author is only to offer information of a general nature to help
you in your quest for emotional and spiritual well-being. In the event you use
any of the information in this book for yourself, which is your constitutional
right, the author and the publisher assume no responsibility for your actions.

Any people depicted in stock imagery provided by Thinkstock are models,
and such images are being used for illustrative purposes only.
Certain stock imagery © Thinkstock.

Edited by Diana Fairbank

Printed in the United States of America.

ISBN: 978-1-4525-2226-5 (sc)
ISBN: 978-1-4525-2228-9 (hc)
ISBN: 978-1-4525-2227-2 (e)

Library of Congress Control Number: 2014916461

Balboa Press rev. date: 09/26/2014

Contents

Introduction

The months and years are zooming by so quickly that I picture the pages of the calendar flipping over and over like in the old black and white films from the 1940's. Here we are, well into the 21st Century in a world that is changing as quickly as those calendar pages. Technology is changing the way we think and our ways of functioning in the world. Now most everyone is comfortably surfing the web for everything that they could possibly want to know or buy; you may have even bought this book on the internet. Science is giving us new information that is expanding our understanding of the so-called "real" world beyond previously held beliefs toward a new interpretation of what *reality itself* is. Quantum physics has opened up a new picture of reality that includes the role of consciousness and matter interacting in ways that suggest that we, as conscious human beings, are participating in the creation of reality along with unseen energy forces such as gravity, electromagnetic fields, etc.

The Law of Attraction seems to have a lot in common with some of the new understanding of science. A view of the universe is emerging that sees all of the components of the universe, including atoms, people and stars, as part of a wholeness or Oneness.

Baby boomers, and members of generations X, and Y, and the Millennials, are awakening to new ideas that have come out of quantum physics, as well as the teachings of abundance consciousness; philosophies that collectively are pushing the boundaries of our beliefs about who we really are, and how the universe works. Together, we are now poised in a pivotal position in history, as we participate in the paradigm shift from a world view of separateness to a world view of Oneness.

Meanwhile, the world population has reached 7 billion people who are putting enormous pressure on the living systems of our planet. Our understanding of the impact of human activities has grown along with the new technologies that allow us to see the planet from space. Satellite photos show us the impact of massive deforestation, strip mining, and desertification for what they really are. Thanks to Google Earth, anybody can view a little spot of ground somewhere in the world from their home computer – you can zoom in on your own home and check out your garden, or you can count the junked cars in your neighbor's back yard.

Our understanding of planet Earth is increasing rapidly through the explosion of communication methods and the internet. Now, interviews with ground-breaking physicists can be viewed on YouTube, any day of the week. With our awareness expanding scientifically, and spiritually, we find ourselves in a paradox: is the reality on planet Earth limited or is it part of an infinite "reality" that we are creating with the collective mind? Personally, I've shifted back and forth between the two world views most of my life and the internal dialog continues. This dilemma provokes questions such as these:

- Are we living on a planet with a limited supply of stuff that we are quickly running out of?
- Are we going to have to go to another planet some day to get more stuff?
- Are we despoiling our habitat with full knowledge of what we are doing and doing it anyway? Really?
- Is our species locked into a behavior pattern that resembles the classic ecological example of a booming population of one species that eventually overgrazes its habitat, leading to collapse?

Or, from the other perspective:

- Is the universe an abundant, ever-expanding creation that is accurately described as "infinite"?
- Do we live in a dynamic universe where everything responds to consciousness?
- Do we indeed create our reality with our thoughts and actions?
- Can we change the direction that our society is taking us?

As Chinese philosopher, Lao Tsu once said:

"If you do not change direction, you may end up where you are heading".

I believe that it is possible to change the direction our society is heading using a process that I call Simple Abundance. This process acknowledges the predicament that our planet is in after several centuries of heavy use by humans, but embraces what abundance consciousness professes, and what the revelations from quantum physics has shown us: that the universe is infinite and co-creative. My own personal awareness and seeking has revealed the connection between science and spirituality that confirms my belief that we create our own reality, moment by moment, in a very malleable universe. Living life in a Simply Abundant way means that we can walk the Earth in a gentle manner, while awakening to the inherent abundance of the universe, and our creative role in shaping the fabric of reality. Ultimately, I believe that we will have a much bigger role in the co-creative process as we discover our true natural abilities in shaping reality. There will be more on that as you read on.

The goal of this book is to reconcile the ideological differences between abundance consciousness and the ecological/environmental realities facing the planet at this time. At first, they seem to be two subjects that are mutually exclusive – how can we possibly believe that the Earth is finite and infinite at the same time? Early in life, I began thinking about these apparently conflicting topics while reading books about abundance consciousness that spoke of human beings' innate ability to create whatever they desired in life. I searched for books that spoke of the power of the subconscious mind, ESP (extrasensory perception), psycho kinesis, astral travel, and whatever else I could find at the time. I kept Joseph Murphy's book, *The Power of the Subconscious Mind*, on my bookshelf throughout high school when most everyone else was focusing on sex, drugs, and rock-n-roll. My interest in abundance consciousness during the 1970's coincided closely with my concern for the environment around us. I joined the Wilderness Society, and participated in Earth Day events, and embraced the philosophy of Deep Ecology. My mind was torn about the apparent conflict between two belief systems: one that envisioned an infinitely abundant universe, most of which was non-physical and beyond my understanding, and a second philosophy that was right in front of my eyes – a fragile world that was straining under the weight of an exponentially expanding human population.

For a while, the idea of abundance consciousness took the back seat; it just didn't sit well with me when I saw the clearing of forests and the paving of farmland as more and more houses spread out across the Midwestern landscape of my youth. In my thinking, I wondered: what if the billions of people on the planet were all hot on the idea of having redwood siding on their houses? How could the planet even support that? In the case of the Sequoia sempervirons, the coast redwood, all of the remaining redwoods in California would have to be cut down; every single last one! Even then, most of the people wouldn't get their redwood siding - the population of redwood trees on the planet just would not support that. And for many generations afterward there would be no old growth redwood forests at all; the only thing left of the ancient, majestic groves of trees would be the memories and photographs of those amazing giants that used to be. What kind of world would that be?

We live in a time when the human impact on the planet has reached immense proportions. For example, humans now consume around half of the entire biological production of the planet for our sole purposes. The fact that one species of organism on the planet is usurping that much of the biosphere's output, often at the expense of millions of other species, raises an ethical challenge. But now, we can ask ethical questions of ourselves, because the human population has evolved enough to examine our place in this world among the multitudes of other beings that we share the planet with. Additionally, we have the capability of high speed computers to model the world of the future and share that information collectively and globally.

Along with the ethical questions are the philosophical questions about what exactly is the nature of *Nature*. What is the fabric of the universe that we live in? I think it is in the examination of these questions that we will find the answers to ethical questions about what role humans have on this planet as well as our place in the universe. Is the reality of the universe a "work in progress"? Can people shape that reality? Is our mere existence shaping that reality? Is every thought and every action shaping the universe?

Eventually, I began to study how quantum physics was changing our concepts about the fabric of the universe itself, and I rediscovered the abundant and creative forces at work in the universe. I came to understand that abundance consciousness and a deep concern for planet Earth go hand in hand. I began to **love** more and experience more **joy** in my life and appreciate the **beauty** of nature in boundless quantities. That's when I realized that those things are infinite – love, joy, and beauty are completely without limits in our universe. Then I started to see my role in creating those things in my world and realized my direct participation in the creative process that I was experiencing as "reality". In my professional life, and in my personal life, I am creating love, and joy, and beauty all of the time. As a professional landscape architect for the past 30 years, I have created outdoor spaces where people can interact with nature, and find happiness in the fresh air and abundance of nature. Every time I walk out my front door and just smile at another human being, I see the creation process at work. Just like the spiritual teachers of ancient and modern times have said: we are participating in the creation of the universe along with Source/God. It took a number of years for me to come to the realization that the two philosophies: abundance conscious and living gently on a small planet were not mutually exclusive topics. Both fields are all about living in harmony and balance; living a centered, peaceful life; connecting with other people and other beings; and being aligned with nature.

So this book is written for people who are spiritually inclined <u>and</u> have a deep connection with Mother Earth. This book is written for people who see themselves as environmentalists <u>and</u> have a thirst to understand more about the mysterious nature of the universe. I think we are the same people in both cases; I know I am. A new world view of abundance and connectedness challenges the old paradigm, just as the astronomical discoveries of Galileo and Copernicus challenged the European beliefs of their time, and thus changed forever the world view of our place in the universe.

What is abundance? Webster's Dictionary calls abundance: "A fullness or plenteousness great to overflowing; ample sufficiency; copiousness, plentiful, ample, fully sufficient, abounding". So, is our world/planet abundant? It seems so. This is a fundamental question that I have been pondering for most of my life. I look at the natural world and see that Nature is constantly creating new life. This is most easily observed when land is devastated by a fire or construction clearing. New plants pop up immediately - "weeds" as we call them, but abundant plant life nonetheless. It seems that abundance is a natural attribute of the Earth. The first chapter of this book looks at the abundant qualities of our home planet.

The nature of the universe itself is abundance. The billions of stars, and billions of galaxies, give testimony to that on a really large scale. Chapter 2 explores the macro level of the universe and the abundance that fills a clear night sky with more stars and galaxies than can be counted. If ever the idea of infinity were to be understood, it would be in the context of the universe which extends out beyond our sight.

The microscopic scale of subatomic particles is also a realm of abundance and connectedness. Chapter 3 summarizes the basics of quantum mechanics in the subatomic world. This book has no intention of proving or disproving theories that have been put forth by some of the most brilliant scientists of all time (Planck, Einstein, Bohr). Physicists themselves often don't agree on all theories. I am certainly not a physicist, but I am deeply intrigued by the microscopic world, and the energy forces that drive the universe. In this book we will take the position of David Bohm (author of *Wholeness and the Implicate Order*), and others, who have postulated our universe is based on wholeness and not separateness.

Every scientist who comes close to understanding the bizarre subatomic world of quantum mechanics has to go home at night, and have dinner with their family, just like the rest of us. They may better understand the nature of reality, but they still need to wash the dishes at the end of the evening. All of us live in a physical environment that we interact with every day, and there are a lot of us who are extremely concerned about the condition of that physical environment. Chapter 4 reviews the state of the everyday world today with sobering thoughts and some visionary ideas.

Chapter 5 then critiques the society of separateness that got us into this mess to begin with. It is this ideology of separateness that is at the root of nearly every problem our world faces today.

This chapter also shows us humankind's ongoing exploration of alternatives that point to the social evolution of our species.

Our continued exploration of new thinking will open us to a new understanding of the Universe that is abundant beyond our imagination. Mysteries continue to intrigue our species, but I think we now have enough of the pieces of the puzzle to put into action the transformation of reality as we know it, toward a reality of peace, love, and prosperity. Chapter 6 examines the beliefs of abundance consciousness.

But our society seems so far from embracing abundance consciousness and a vision of unity right now – look at politics in the United States! In Chapter 7, many connections will be made between where we are now in the state of the world, and where we need to go, in terms of Oneness. What everyone seems to want in life comes down to some basic needs that are shared by all humans of all cultures, all nations, all political orientations, genders, etc. We want love, peace and joy. Meeting these basic needs underlies most of the greatest achievements of humanity, and causes many of our shortcomings, as well. This chapter shows ways that people are far more connected than separated today, and some of the trends that are moving us toward Oneness.

Chapter 8 introduces the new philosophy of being Simply Abundant: a philosophy that merges abundance consciousness with living simply. When people attend abundance seminars and speak of wanting more money in their lives, they don't really want trunks filled with dollar bills, not really. What they innately want are the experiences, and feelings, that would come along with having that much money. Knowing that the universe is an abundant field of creative energy gives us the opportunity to have everything that we really want in our lives - love, peace, harmony, family, community, health, nourishment, security, prosperity, freedom, happiness, liberty, and creative expression. These experiences in life are abundant in every sense of the word. We can have as much of those that we need, want or desire, and there are specific steps to take to create those experiences in our lives.

There are practical considerations in life, of course. Just how does this philosophy of living Simply Abundant apply in real life conditions? In Chapter 9, we will take some examples of real life situations, and apply the principles of Simple Abundance to ground the ideas that were discussed in the previous chapters.

Chapter 10 is a plan of action to change the world. That's right; our intention must be nothing less than changing the world! With the recognition that we humans are active participants in the creation of reality as we know it, we have the opportunity to create the reality that we desire. There is much work to be done to arrive at global consensus about what humanity desires, but ultimately, I suggest that our collective conscious desires peace, love, joy, and prosperity. I say this with a high degree of confidence that deep in our hearts all people desire the same thing for our species and our planet. So, please read on, and join me in creating the paradigm shift that will be the result of our intention and conscious thoughts.

Acknowledging that some aspects of our current lifestyle are not sustainable in our present reality, we need to live appropriately. Even though at our core, every human is a creator of immense capabilities, we have a long way to go to master the art of manifesting physical elements. Seven billion people cannot go straight into moving mountains under the current state of reality;

there would be a traffic jam of mountains going here and there –
we could call it *Mount Rush Hour*. The vision of human beings
as alchemists is definitely in our future, but first things first:
the manifestation necessary to meet human needs, and guard
the planet's health. Then, we can move on to our *true* nature as
Beings: co-creators of reality, along with Source.

I will refer often to Source, Source energy, Universal Source field,
or Oneness, which are all terms that I use interchangeably, that
refer to the great creative power that exists. Call that creative
power God if you like; I will, at times. But I try not to use words
that are too culturally burdened, in an effort to keep our minds
open. When I capitalize a word such as Universe I am referring
to the powerful Divine energy that creates reality vs. the physical
matter of the universe (in lower case). Ultimately, all is connected,
and one of the same, but for the purposes explained in this book,
that is how I intend the words to read.

There is something for everyone in this book, but it will take a little
stretching to reach common ground on the ideas of abundance,
and the well-being of Mother Earth. So, we need to stretch a little
to get there, we need to stretch into alignment with the energy of
Earth, and of Source; we need to be Simply Abundant.

CHAPTER 1

The Abundant Planet

**"It is a little planet
But how beautiful it is."**
Robinson Jeffers

We live on a magnificent planet that provides abundant splendor for all of the creatures who live here, as evidenced by the tremendous growth of life on Earth. All around us we see plants and animals thriving and multiplying. Take a long look at a flower some day and marvel at the complexity of the colors and patterns – the crinkles gracing every little petal. In never-ending variety, nature is abundantly creating. Each species is creating new and wonderful ways of expanding and multiplying across all of the lands and oceans. The land itself is expanding as new liquid rock comes spewing up out of island volcanoes and continents slide across the globe on their shifting plates. Nature seems to be in the process of limitless creation. 24/7, as we say.

Earth is in creation mode day and night. However, to our planet there is no day and night - just rotating on its axis and gliding in its orbit, on and on for billions of years. When you think about it, Earth is set to auto-pilot. It's like the controls of the planet are set in terms of gravity and rotation and then the creative energy of nature is set loose on the planet with no limits put on it. Nature seems to have a blank check to create more and more of itself, and an eternity to do it.

When I say "nature", personally, I would include the entire man-made environment in my picture of nature: buildings, streets, cities, machines, etc. Just because humans have constructed them doesn't mean that they aren't natural. It's natural for humans to create, that's just what we do, well, naturally. At Findhorn in the 1960's, Eileen Caddy made contact with the "spirit" of some man-made machines such as a typewriter and an automobile. Ever since learning of machines potentially having consciousness at a certain level, I've tried to stay open minded about that. So, I believe man-made stuff is natural. But in this chapter, I will try to stay focused on the natural world that we are accustomed to picturing: the elements of earth, air, water, fire; the minerals, the plant kingdom; the animal kingdom; and everything in between.

We can witness the abundance of Earth whenever we step outdoors to start our day. From the smallest microbe to the immeasurable wealth of the biosphere itself, abundance can be found. In this book I will explore the abundance of nature with you because I love the natural world. I find it easy to see Source energy at work everywhere I go in nature. This is especially true when the forces of nature are viewed in juxtaposition with the man-made world, such as in a city. My heart really sings when I see a little plant sprouting up in a crack in a concrete sidewalk or asphalt parking lot. People have paved a large surface of this planet it seems – millions of acres of paving just in the United States. But even that doesn't stop these little plants!

Just imagine the zest for life that exists in the dandelion that miraculously finds itself seeded into a crack in the sidewalk. Here is this little dormant seed that wakes up when a little water leaks into the crack. Does the little seed say to itself: "oh shit, I'm in a crack! I get all the bad luck"? Probably not. Little seed just gets to work, most likely doing what he does best – grow. These are the ubiquitous seeds we all know famously from our childhood of blowing the seeds joyfully to the wind. I remember making a wish and then trying to blow all the seeds off of the dandelion flower in one breath, thus accomplishing a small feat of lung power. The sail of the dandelion seed would carry it quite some distance which was another joy to a young boy: to see how far a seed would fly before hitting the ground. The seed might fly for hundreds of feet under the right conditions; sometimes right into the yard of a neighbor who might be cursing dandelions (and little kids) next spring. However, the dandelion seed we are following today flies along and then skips along the sidewalk and tumbles into a crack in the concrete where he sits for a while.

The dandelion is a dicot, which is a very broad category of vascular plants, including most shrubs and trees, which produce dicotyledonous seeds. The dicotyledon seed is divided into two halves which simultaneously send out two stems, one that becomes the plant's top, and a second stem that is the beginning of the root system. Our little dandelion seed, once it busts open and starts sending out those stems, begins its next phase of life. The new plant uses the stored energy of the seed to feed the growth of its roots and leaves. Before its stored energy is depleted, it is essential that the root reaches something that resembles soil, and the leaves need to reach the open air, and begin receiving sunlight for photosynthesis. Once photosynthesis is underway, the plant starts to produce its own food and can supply its developing root system. So, here is this little plant that is dividing its energy between root growth and leaf growth and collectively pushing up, and pushing down through the crack. Lo, and behold, the root reaches some rocky soil that the roots can wrap around and the leaves reach the surface of the sidewalk where the Sun shines most of the time. The persistence of our dandelion is inspirational. He might live long enough to put out a green mass of leaves and a big yellow flower with dozens more of the little seeds for kids to blow.

All around our planet we find the persistence of nature working away on its task of creation, from the tiniest microbe, to the vast movements of continents. With a small amount of observation, evidence of abundance here on Earth can be seen and appreciated every day, everywhere.

Whenever I spend time in the wilds, I marvel at the abundance of the natural world. While on long hikes in the mountains, I often have many hours of staring at the trail directly in front of my feet. Once I'm in the groove of the hiking pace but focused enough to avoid tripping, I let my eyes wander into the forest and I allow my mind to contemplate my connection to the universe. The land seems to speak to me of its history. The story tells of the rising of the mountains due to the shifting plate tectonics and the lowering of the mountains by the incessant rain that falls and the rivers that flow. The soil is formed from the rocks that are ground to dust by the water, and the rocky soil supports the few little plants whose seeds are brought by the wind, or dropped by birds. Like our little dandelion, each plant has a mission to grow and multiply - to create.

The pioneer plants have their role to play in the early years of forest life, only to be replaced by others. Then bigger plants take root, and wave after wave of plant species come and go in the plant community. Ecologists call it *succession*, and after a while, the community is a forest.

The trees have their story to tell of life and death. For thousands of years these tree communities have lived in the mountains. Winds knock down the giant grandfather trees whose trunks then become the nursery for the little grandchildren seedlings. Fallen hemlocks are famous for this nurse log behavior, each downed log supporting the sprouts of dozens of little seedlings. The mature conifer tree, hemlock, fir, pine, can produce up to 10,000 cones on its branches in the course of a year. The weight of the cones pulls the branches down like children clinging to the arms of their mommies and daddies. The fir cones point upward in the fashion unique to their species. The pine and other conifers have cones that dangle downward aiming toward the target – the soil. These trees have a destiny that they seem eager to fulfill. The world's largest cones belong to the Coulter pines native to California. Their cones measure up to 15 inches long and can weigh 10 lbs. or more. Hikers in the Coast Ranges, beware of falling cones! The seeds of the conifer cones take up to two years to ripen completely, and then they eventually begin to split, seeds individuate, and drop off the cone. Every cone contains dozens of seeds. Each year, a tree can produce enough seeds to reproduce itself thousands of times over, and in its lifetime, a conifer tree will have produced enough seeds to reproduce itself millions of times. Those trees' reproductive habits speak of abundance.

In a redwood forest recently, I saw the clumps of redwoods, young and old grouped together in crowded clusters. Some of those redwoods were several feet in diameter, and hundreds of years old; some were skinny poles of modest height, and some were only seedlings. But they were all reaching for the sky and the limited light of the dense forest. Each tree seemed to be saying: "I want a chance to live here too!" Trees love to live in community with each other, and other species.

All around us in the forest, we see abundance. Once trees are established they provide living space for ever more species: lichen clings to the bark, moss drips from the branches, bugs climb up and down, birds peck at the wood, and nest where they can. There are a number of ways to portray relationships in nature, and lots of people prefer the Darwinian view of "survival of the fittest", because it seems to justify human aggressive tendencies that appear to be natural. However, there are many other models of nature to consider. I prefer to think of nature as an extended family of species making the best of the vibrant quality of Earth. Each species is creating its niche and advancing its desire to live and create.

Symbiosis is the word that describes the relationship between two or more species that live together and interact with each other in the same place. Picture various unrelated people living and getting along in the same house. Maybe they are not only just "getting along" but also helping each other to prosper. Symbiotic relationships tend to be classified as mutually beneficial to all parties when the species benefit from the relationship with each other, such as the carp that clean the teeth of hippopotamuses in rivers and lakes of Africa. The hippos lower themselves down in the water and then open their huge mouths for the fish to swim in. These fish provide the much needed dental service in exchange for some choice morsels that are offered up by the hippos. It is a mutually beneficial relationship for all involved.

Sure, there are parasitic relationships in nature just like in human society – like the numerous evil "bad guys" that populate American films. We, people, tend to focus on negative or parasitic relationships, and make movies about them. But in nature, the cooperative relations outnumber the parasitic ones by far, and we haven't even discovered all of the naturally beneficial relationships yet.

We are seeing evidence that our planet of living and non-living Beings are connected and cooperating. The science of systems ecology shows us that complex inter-related systems are the basis for our planet's function. The Gaia Hypothesis, as developed by James Lovelock and Lynn Margolis, gives us a picture of how living systems on Earth are working together in ways to make the planet habitable for all of us.

Planet Earth can be seen as a whole organism itself, with each species or group, a subset. The idea of one thing being a subset of a larger whole makes perfect sense in biology and other sciences. Each strand of DNA is part of the double helix, which forms the gene, which forms the chromosome, which is part of a cell. The cell is part of the tissue that makes up a muscle that makes up a limb or organ that is part of you. Therefore, each cell in our body is an individual entity and a component of the larger being of You. The human body is a community of 50 trillion cells living and working and creating in a joint venture together.

There are systems all over the place in nature. A little plant doesn't just sit out there all by himself without any friends. Individual plants join with others of their own kind and with other species to form plant communities. Groups of plants and animals living together form communities that interact with each other and become ecosystems. Ecosystems interacting together form the biosphere, and on and on. Everything is part of something else, which is part of something else even bigger. Life is like an infinite collection of Russian nesting dolls.

For me it's exciting and comforting to know that I personally am part of something larger. At the scale of societies, that is probably the motivation for clubs, congregations, and nationalism, here in our country: the human need to be part of something larger. So here we are folks, on the verge of something really big; we now all have memberships in the Human Being Club. We are of course, genetically, one species of beings here: human beings, Homo sapiens sapiens beings - people. Our little club though, has the opportunity to be part of a much bigger club: Gaia, or we could call it the Congregation of Earth Beings. How cool is that?

Imagine the possibilities of humans working with their neighbor species to learn the best way to live together. With our enormous human intelligence collaborating with the joint intelligence of all the other species, think of what can be accomplished. I see paradise!

The intelligence of nature is beyond our current understanding, to be sure, but the Source of all Creation is everywhere. Try taking a magnifying glass out into the forest and viewing the life that is happening unnoticed to the casual glace. A simple moss patch might have many species of moss and lichen and fungus and bugs. With a microscope, the observable life is multiplied by at least a few factors of ten. It boggles the mind to think that in every cubic centimeter of forest soil live thousands of bacteria organisms. Bacteria are, in fact, everywhere in the biosphere. They are inside our stomachs, in the atmosphere, in the soil, underground, in the ocean, under the ocean. What's the total population of bacteria in this world? Estimates are that it is 10^{31}, which is a number with a <u>lot</u> of zeros. As in this many: 10,000,000,000,000,000,000, 000,000,000,000. Microbiologists acknowledge that this is only an approximation, because new bacteria are being found in new places all the time.

For an eye-popping experience of abundance in nature without a microscope, take a good look at the community of mushrooms in the fall forest duff, or in your backyard, under the crispy fall leaves. You don't have to be a mycological expert to know that there is something magical going on in the mushroom world come October. They are everywhere on the forest floor, or lawn, or roadside ditch, or almost anywhere after the first fall rain, and before the first snow. Go for a walk in the park and feast your eyes on an extraordinary display of colors, shapes and textures as the fungus world goes into its reproductive phase. That's what those cute buttons are up to in the fall, of course - reproduction. You see, the mushroom cap is the vessel that contains the spores that fungus "spawn". The mushroom cap is the reproductive organ of an enormous underground organism that lives unseen beneath our feet. The mushroom organism is better described as a vast fibrous network that spreads out underground intertwined with soil, plant roots and everything else down there. So vast is its fibrous network, that the lil 'ol mushroom can claim the title of **Largest Living Organism** on the planet. Some mushroom fibers from a single organism can cover several acres of land. The largest one is a 'shroom that covers 2,200 acres of land in Oregon. This isn't hundreds of mushrooms all interconnected underground, genetically, this is <u>one</u> organism.

When you stop, sit down and really notice them, mushrooms are truly amazing. They may be a fraction of an inch long or two feet wide. Their color schemes include: pure white, black with speckles, grey, dark purple, fire-engine red, brown striped, polka-dot orange, yellow, beige, and even green. They can be shiny, dull, wrinkled, or spiky. Mushrooms push their lumpy round heads up through the forest duff of leaves, moss, and debris in a matter of hours - so fast that if you paused long enough, you could watch them bumping aside soil and leaves to get their heads above ground. They pop up out the ground in pairs, small groups, large crowded colonies, or all by themselves. Upon close examination though, the mushrooms that seem to be alone are often in a line or circle (the legendary "fairy circles") with others that mirror the fibers below the surface. All this work is carefully orchestrated by an underground intelligence that we don't fully understand. We just know the mushroom by the miniscule part that pops up for a few days while its main, fibrous body lays quietly below the leaves on the October ground.

Hiking is a good time for meditations on life. We tend to call our time in nature by other names such as: outdoor recreation or adventure sports to commercialize hiking, climbing, kayaking, skiing, etc. But it is really about communing with nature and most people will acknowledge that, upon reflection. You don't have to go far, though, to connect with nature. Every day there are opportunities to experience the abundance of the natural world.

I was sitting on my deck one day enjoying some late summer sun when a green tinged Ruby- throated Hummingbird zipped past me to hover over a potted plant. That's not that special, you could say, because they're fairly common, and the little guy only hovered for a few seconds. But, for me, it was magical, and it was made possible thanks to my Simply Abundant life. It takes very little effort to appreciate a hummingbird; they're cute, fascinating, and they can just show up on a moment's notice; you just have to take notice.

Sitting in the sun (which is not guaranteed in my part of the world) is a marvel and witness to Simple Abundance. The radiant heat washes over my body and is absorbed into my skin. The hum of the rapidly flapping wings of the hummingbird is music to my ears. The smell of fresh salty air blowing in from the Puget Sound triggers memories of various salt-water experiences dating back to childhood. The puffy white marshmallow clouds grace the horizon. All of this abundant sensual pleasure is available to me in my state of awareness of the infinite nature of Creation. I experience it through my five senses, but also in my soul, I feel connected to nature through unseen vibrations.

Living Simply Abundant allows one to connect with nature through the senses, and then into a deeper vibrational level below the threshold of consciousness, into the super-conscious. Because at the deeper levels, we know we're connected to all things in the universe. By seeing the infinite abundance of nature and knowing that we humans are connected to it all gives us permission to become one with nature and the universe. This makes us abundant and infinite, and just like nature, human thought is ever-expanding. We can celebrate that truth standing right where we are on Earth.

Who is not in awe of the exuberant growth that surges forth each spring? It is no wonder that so many cultures celebrate spring in some way. The dense upward push of species after species of plants that accompanies warm weather in the springtime is testimony to abundance in nature. The quest for sunlight and water that all plants pursue is relentless. I've always enjoyed watching roots grow from seed or from starts in little pots or cups in my kitchen window. The roots seem to be saying to the leaves: "OK leaves, you go for the sunlight and I'll go for the water and we'll feed each other as we go".

Water, in all its forms, is abundant when considering that 70% of the planet is covered by water in the form of seas, lakes, rivers, and ice. The sky, too, is filled with water in the clouds that swirl above our continents, and oceans, in a never-ending array of globe-trotting magnificence. Underground, sometimes only a few feet down, is water in flowing aquifers in places all over the Earth. Hydro geologists say that rivers and lakes are really just the surface expressions of the water table which lies beneath the soil. All of the water underground, in the atmosphere, and on the surface comprises the hydrosphere – over one billion cubic kilometers of water.

The sight of water making a transition from aquifer to the surface is one of the most fantastic wonders of nature - a spring. The water just comes bubbling up right out of the ground from a little hole or a crack between rocks. Sometimes, the hole is not so little and the source of water is significant. North central Florida, southern Idaho, and the Ozark region in the United States are known for major natural springs. The porous rock formations allow water to move to the surface in great quantities. Big Springs in Missouri releases over 1,000,000 cubic meters of water per day. My favorite spring is the Fontaine-de-Vaucluse in Provence, France. This one is one of the largest in the world and flows at nearly 2,000,000 cubic meters of water per day creating the River Sorgue as it goes. That volume is only two cubic kilometers out of the one billion cubic kilometers of the hydrosphere but still, it is quite the flow – picture about 70,000 garden hoses all going full on. Springs have held mystical interest for people since ancient times. Roman coins from 100BCE have been found hundreds of feet deep in the Fontaine-de-Vaucluse, undoubtedly tossed by Romans and locals and accompanied with a wish. Note: appropriately, the word for spring in French is *source*.

Human Beings are water too. By weight, we are somewhere between 50-75% water in our cells, blood, tissues, and muscles. This could be why we are so linked to that marvelous molecule. The functions of the body depend on water for proper muscle movements, processing of food, and brain operations like thinking. People feel good when they are around water. Coastlines, lakes, rivers, springs, and waterfalls are all popular destinations to visit or live. In fact, most people on Earth live within a few miles of water out of necessity, but also out of the pure joy from being in proximity to water. Picture yourself right now next to a beautiful waterfall with clean, fresh water cascading off the rocks, and splashing into a pool. You may even have a favorite waterfall that you have hiked to in the mountains. It doesn't take much to allow good feelings to come into your mind when thinking about a splendid waterfall, in a natural setting surrounded by trees, and ferns, and mossy rocks. Part of our connection with water and nature is biological or biochemical and part of our connection is spiritual. Earth is our home; it is part of us and we are part of it.

As I write this I am watching a storm roll in from the Pacific Ocean and spill into the Puget Sound basin. Safely behind my living room window, I see wind whipped waves forming white caps in Elliott Bay. The spindrift is flying off the wave crests and splashing into the waves behind which march on toward the shore in an endless parade. So I ask myself: is the wind abundant?

Certainly, today, it is! Steel chairs on the deck are getting blown over. The winds of planet Earth certainly seem abundant.

The wind must seem abundant enough to the engineers and utility planners who are helping wind power to be established in the ranks of legitimate energy sources. Truly abundant and infinitely renewable is what makes wind power so attractive to the renewable energy community of private companies, municipal utilities, environmental activists, and farmers. Farmers stand to gain considerably from wind power as a reliable way of supplementing their fluctuating incomes year to year from their crops. By now many of us have seen wind "farms" of multiple turbines slowly rotating in corn fields or pastures with cows grazing nearby. Massive wind farms in Texas, western New York, and California have made wind-generated electricity competitive with other forms of electric power from conventional sources. Al Gore in his book, *Our Choice,* gives the examples of Minnesota, Iowa, and Colorado that have also developed wind power to the point that wind now provides more that 5% of the electricity generated in each of those states (Gore, p. 90). Wind machines are a beautiful sight to any environmentally-minded person who uses electricity for so many practical things.

Europeans, ever-creative in making practical use of their crowded corner of the Eurasian continent, have placed wind turbines all over their countryside. Germany has taken the lead in technology, while Denmark and Great Britain have constructed many wind platforms off shore in the North Sea. In Holland, quaintly known for their windmills of course, the Dutch have placed wind machines in industrial and port districts; I could see the blades turning from my hotel window on my last visit to Amsterdam in 2009.

Coastlines are notoriously windy because the air temperature difference between the land mass and the ocean mass almost guarantees winds. This is why coastal areas and offshore platforms have so much potential. Since the majority of the world's people live on coastlines, wind power could be a very big deal in generating electricity in those locations. There is something about using an old fashioned idea like windmills and updating the technology for the current age that is really appealing. It's like seeing a boat that is powered by the wind with billowing sails and remembering that the wind has powered boats and ships for a <u>long</u> time.

Windmill technology is well known and the engineering necessary for efficiency has taken great strides in recent years. Production of wind machine blades and turbines is similar to that of the aerospace industry, and the equipment is easily mass-produced. Clean, inexhaustible wind energy is right here in abundance. Of course one of the limitations to wind power is that there are limited places where the wind is significant enough; places with a constant wind speed over 15 mph, for example. But the source itself is as close to infinite as can be obtained on planet Earth. Wind here on the planet's surface is just another fringe benefit of our ever-burning Sun that warms our planet. Because of the Earth's tilted axis, and dozens of other factors, the Sun warms the Earth very unevenly. Frozen tundra, steamy rainforests, warm tropical seas, and frigid arctic waters are all part of life on this planet. So, as long as the Sun keeps shining on us, and the Earth's surface temperatures keep fluctuating from one place to the next, wind will be with us, pretty much forever.

It's easy to see all the stuff happening on the Earth's surface like the forests, windy coastlines, and gritty soil surface. But below all of that is a vast world that we hardly think about at all.

The deepest inside the Earth that most people see is down into a cave several feet below the surface, although miners regularly venture several hundred feet down to tap a vein of some mineral. Deep down into the crust of the planet is a domain reserved for geologists and even they don't have a completely clear picture beyond a few miles down. The depth to the center of the Earth is actually several thousand miles. Wow, hardly anyone besides Jules Verne ever thinks about this enormous unexplored region of planet Earth. Here we are going up and out to other planets and we don't know what's down in the middle of our own planet!

Geologists think that the center of the Earth is a ball of molten hot metal such as iron at temperatures up to 12,000 degrees F. The outer mantle of the Earth is also extremely hot (2000 - 6000 degrees F). Even the near-surface crust of the globe has temperatures as hot as 400-1000 degrees F at a depth of only a few miles (Gore, p. 105). No wonder ideas of flaming Hades and burning Hell were (are) so common among the various religions.

Well, a few miles is still a long way down, so geothermal energy has only been captured in the few hot spots close to the surface. Iceland warms most of their homes and some of their office buildings with geothermal heat from water that just bubbles right to the surface. Yep, hot springs, all over Iceland! The Icelandic people, in commonality with Californians, love hot springs. Not surprisingly, one of the largest American geothermal developments is in Northern California.

In California, and Iceland, as well as New Zealand, Indonesia, Japan, the Philippines, Nicaragua, El Salvador, Costa Rica, and Kenya there are efforts toward using geothermal heat for electrical production using turbines. Just like wind power, turbines are being used with steam in geothermal plants to generate electricity, so the technology is definitely here.

The enormous potential of geothermal power is a little hard to fathom; just like it is hard to fathom the fact that the inhabitants of our planet are actually living on the thin cool crust of a molten hot burning ball of fire flying through space. And we've inhabited this fertile crust all these millions of years and the planet doesn't seem to be cooling down one bit. This planet has been a furnace of stored heat for billions of years. Geothermal heat from our own planet is abundant beyond just about anyone's imagination.

Gore, in his book, points out that most people dismiss geothermal power as an answer to the energy needs of our society because they associate geothermal with the limited number of sites where the hot water is very close to the surface - Iceland, for example. The real potential of geothermal power is at depths in the range of 3-5 miles deep where the temperatures are consistently above 400 degrees F. Three to five miles deep sounds really deep. However, the petroleum extraction industry is already in the practice of drilling to depths of 5-6 miles deep for oil and natural gas. These petroleum engineers have developed lots of techniques for deep drilling that could transfer to the much more sustainable and cleaner energy source of geothermal heat. Gore's sources say that "within the outer six miles of the Earth's crust is estimated to contain 50,000 times as much energy as all of the petroleum and natural gas reserves in the world". (Gore, page 105).

What that means is, that using technology that humans have already developed, for the most part, we can tap into an unimaginably large heat source that has been cooking unseen beneath our feet for billions of years and will continue to cook for billions more to come. Abundant, yes. Unlimited, just about. It's true that the planet itself has a lifespan that will be somewhat shorter than that of our Sun – we have a few more billion years left here. The definition of unlimited in this book refers to that timeframe, the life of the Sun, whose life is estimated to be about half over, but still has billions of years to go.

The resource of geothermal energy is so incredibly abundant, and plentiful that it is laughable that we 21st-Century humans are still even considering expanding nuclear power, which currently depends on a rare mineral, Uranium that stays radioactively poisonous for hundreds of thousands of years. Well, that situation isn't really laughable; it truly qualifies as insane.

Our planet is abundant beyond our ability to recognize it. That's part of the problem: humans don't seem to be able to see the big picture and recognize abundance when it's right under our feet. Simple Abundance allows us to recognize the abundance of our planet and dial into all that abundance that the Earth offers without making a mess of things.

What about gravity - that abundant energy force that pervasively shapes everything we do on this planet? What if we could figure out a way to utilize the ever-present force of gravity to our advantage? One might ask: but how? Think about the trains that use matching ends of magnets to defy gravity and lift the trains slightly above the tracks, allowing them to travel with much less friction. If we let our minds run with some of these ideas, we'll be surprised at the incredible solutions we find.

Much of what the Earth has to offer is a result of the creation of the Sun, and the solar system, about 5 billion years ago.

The Sun is abundant beyond the miniscule range of human comprehension. That's also a problem: we humans need to expand our comprehension of the universe. The Sun has been shining for five billion years and will keep shining for billions of years into the future. The amount of energy that the Sun casts out across the solar system is incredibly vast and only a minute fraction of that radiation even lands on our planet. Although it is just a small fraction of the Sun's energy it is estimated to be is enough energy to meet the entire power needs of our developed world many times over. We'll talk more about the Sun in the next chapter, but for now, we can assuredly say: the Sun = abundance.

As in many industries, China is leading the world in solar equipment production, which is driving the costs down. Germany, as always, is on the leading edge in Europe, and is supplying increasing amounts of solar power each year. Solar industries are starting to take off here in the United States as Amy Larkin shows in her book, *Environmental Debt, The Hidden Costs of A Changing Global Economy*, and in 2011 employed about 100,000 people. Therefore, solar power prices are dropping quickly, and the industry is doubling in size every four years (Larkin, p. 130).

People have been in awe of nature from the beginning of humankind's first conscious thoughts (whenever that was). In our ancient past, we have looked out at oceans that stretched as far as one could see and thought that they have no end. We can see mountains that go on and on to the distant horizon and vast quiet deserts that seem to swallow people up. Rainforests in the Amazon basin and the taiga forests of the far north lead you to believe that those trees go on forever also.

But you say: ah! - we know better now; we know those places on Earth are limited. We have Google Earth to show us satellite images of our little planet and we can zoom in on clear cuts in remote (or not so remote) forests. We can take a virtual flight over the suburban expanses that extend out from major cities and see for ourselves that human habitation is out of control! Right? We'll get to that train of thought in another chapter, but for now we can say that our planet is both strong and fragile; both abundant and limited. The question mainly rests on the level of observation. Fortunately, we can take a look at this question from several levels. We have microscopic technology that helps us to understand things from a different perspective and scientists who, themselves, are looking at science differently. We have satellite images to show us what our planet looks like from space - a little blue gem floating in an endless vastness of space. One planet, many species, all connected. And we look out into space and see our Sun shining in everlasting abundance and countless other suns illuminating the night sky.

So, stay with the thoughts of abundance, as we continue on to expand exponentially our view of the abundance of nature when we take a look at the cosmos.

C H A P T E R 2

The Abundant Universe – Cosmos

**"The surface of the Earth is a shore
of the cosmic ocean."**
Carl Sagan

The Sun is unlimited, the universe is infinite.

For the purposes of what is discussed in this chapter, the star in the center of our solar system, the Sun is considered to be unlimited. The Sun is estimated to be a little less than 5 billion years old, and our solar system of planets, moons, and asteroids were all formed out of the same cosmic cloud that is the origin of the Sun. It is expected that the Sun will become a "red giant" type of star in a few billion years and expand to a size that may consume our planet along with the other inner planets, Mercury and Venus. The Earth may be uninhabitable long before that because the expanding size of the Sun will affect our planet in ways that will make it impossible for life as we know it to continue.

Not to mention the fact that the moon is slowly moving away from Earth; this will eventually (in a few billion years) wreak havoc on the tilt of the axis, the rotation of the Earth and the ocean tides. So, to avoid an excessively long debate about the definition of *unlimited*, we will consider the timeframe of the next several billion years of the Sun's existence to be unlimited.

The universe itself may have a lifespan depending on which cosmology theory you're listening to. Modern cosmologists and astrophysicists have been hotly debating the fate of the universe for several decades and have tried to apply the physical laws that we know to the forces that seem to be driving an expanding universe in an infinite fashion. The newest theories about an expanding universe are busting open the discussion about the fate of our "universe" to include an even bigger picture of reality known as "multiverse". We'll look at the really big picture of the cosmos later on but again, for the purposes of this chapter, we will consider the universe that most people understand today as "our universe" to be infinite.

It is too easy to see the Sun only from the perspective of the surface of our planet. This evening I'm watching a colorful sunset behind the Olympic Mountains from my home in Seattle and thinking that in space, the Sun never actually "sets"...

The ancients thought of the Sun as the divine source of all life, and they were right. The Sun makes all life on Earth possible. All life on land and in the oceans is made possible by the energy delivered by the Sun to planet Earth. The radiation from the Sun is responsible for the warmth of the ocean that produces most of the weather on Earth. Sunlight gives us photosynthesis which in turn gives us almost all of the plant life on the planet. Each plant leaf is a solar collector that catches the rays of the Sun and converts it to chlorophyll that allows the plant to continue to grow. Animals, like us, eat the plants and we grow, etc. All of the abundance in the natural world of our planet is brought to us by the abundance of the Sun.

Our Sun is actually a gigantic nuclear reactor that converts hydrogen atoms to helium atoms in the process of nuclear fusion that creates enormous amounts of energy. The estimated amount of energy that the Sun produces is astronomical and the amount of solar energy landing on our little planet, 93,000,000 miles away, is only about .00000001 % of the energy that the Sun puts out. So powerful are the Sun's rays though, that the seemingly infinitesimal amount of energy is enough energy to power all of modern man's needs many times over. Talk about abundant!

Average people, when they put on their sunglasses to go outside in the summer, don't think that the orange orb in the sky is a gargantuan burning ball of hydrogen gas, hundreds of times larger than Earth, and is itself hurtling through space, with us in orbital tow. Think about it: when we go to sleep at night in darkness, the Sun doesn't take a break - it continues the burning of hydrogen nonstop like it has for billions of years – *nonstop for billions of years*. I say it like this for the main reason of training myself to realize how mind boggling the energy of our Sun really is. I take that energy for granted as I oooou and ahhhh over the vibrant colors of the sunset.

Our solar system of eight or nine planets, a few dozen moons, and millions of asteroids came from the same cloud of cosmic debris that our sun came from about 4-1/2 billion years ago. We have learned a lot more about these planets in the past 30 years of space exploration that began with the Apollo program in the 1960s. Since then, we have put rover vehicles on the surface of Mars and other craft in the orbit taking measurements and samples. Several space probes have been sent out from Earth, including the Voyager I & II to study the outer planets which have sent back lots of new data about Jupiter, Saturn, Uranus, and Neptune. There are new rings of Neptune to see, and two dozen more moons of Uranus and Neptune, that had been previously unknown.

Not that far from Earth are numerous asteroids. And between Mars and Jupiter is the Asteroid Belt, a vast region of space and home to millions of asteroids. I am fascinated with these little mini-planets orbiting the Sun just like us. Of course most asteroids are basically just rocks flying around out there but some are larger, up to 100 kilometers or so, and are rich with minerals and water (ice). Ideas have been floated by scientists and futurists about the possibility of accessing the natural resources of asteroids. There are, it seems enough minerals on nearby asteroids to use to build large space stations in orbit around Earth. The idea of humans living in space is not out of the question in the near future and may be part of the answer to the challenges facing humanity. People have already been living in space at the International Space Station for up to six months at a time.

As a young boy I was always fascinated by the idea of living in space. I saw the first walk on the moon in 1969, and listened to rock music in the 1970s that evoked images of life in space, or on another planet (David Bowie, Pink Floyd). But philosophically, I wrestled with the notion that space colonization was evidence that humans just couldn't solve our problems here on Earth and would soon export all of our deplorable issues into space without fixing anything on Earth. This could end up being a repeat of what the Europeans did when they left that continent for the Americas, Africa and Australia and just brought all their biased programs of violence and exploitation along. The worst of those visions started to come true in the 1980's as the US government tried to militarize space with the "Star Wars" program that gave us the very real possibility of nuclear weapons being placed in low orbit around our planet. What a nightmare.

However, a scenario with humans living in constructed space colonies is not all bad and certainly in the realm of technical possibility. Solar energy is more abundant in space, constant, easier to access, clean, and free. Construction in space is, in many ways, easier than construction on the gravity-restricted Earth's surface. Building materials would be readily available from one of those asteroids that are orbiting in close proximity to Earth. Enormous resources on asteroids like iron and nickel for construction; oxygen and water for life, are available. Land area can be created from soil mined from the asteroids. I know, I know, strip mining asteroids is no better than strip mining Earth, right? Or is it? The idea deserves further thought. On a space colony, living systems, by their very nature would have to be sustainable and every resource would have to be recycled continuously (good lessons to be learned there). Once a space colony is up and running, the ongoing functions can be carried out without further pollution of the Earth's biosphere. This could be like Ecotopia in space!

Hmmm. The prospect definitely resembles a double-edged sword. On one side we have the opportunity to learn how humans can live peacefully and sustainably in space, and on the other hand, people acting from their lowest level of thinking, could turn space into another area of conflict to fight about. Unfortunately, at this point in time, the human race seems stuck in a self-destructive mode. It's hard to believe that a dozen years into the 21st century suicide bombers are still blowing themselves, and others, up in marketplaces around the world.

Visionary thinkers first started planning for space colony construction with asteroid materials and powered by solar power back in the late 1970s. Now, 40 years later (the same time frame envisioned by the early scientists for the first space colonists to start living in space) we are still very much earthbound. But in many ways we've made progress; space shuttles have been moving scientists back and forth from the space station in orbit for quite some time. And the International Space Station is operational proof that humans can work together for a common goal.

People working together on creating peaceful living opportunities in space would be a huge step forward for human kind. Who knows, this could be the end of nationalism, aggression and war. It's worth noting that all of the principle nations who are now working together (United States, Russia, the European Union, Japan, Canada) have been enemies in the past. Certainly a project of human space colonies has the potential to make our petty earthbound issues irrelevant. Nations putting their differences behind them to work together as One, now that's big news. News agencies that prefer reporting on bombing incidents are largely ignoring the "huge leap for humanity" that is taking place in space.

Since the 1970's the idea of space colonization hasn't gotten much press but NASA's Ames Research Center in California has kept the vision alive with annual space colony design competitions. Visit any of the websites that follow that news, including www.NASA. gov - it's inspiring.

Can we create these orbiting space colonies that are sustainable and allow for further expansion into space? Human beings, as creative Beings that we are, have a constant need to expand, all of nature does. Humans could express this natural expansion by replicating space colonies in the orbit of other planets or building settlements on Mars. Who knows? Our limited thinking is a trap that has kept humans from further expansion. The abundance of space awaits humanity's expansive thoughts.

Any discussion about abundance would be incomplete without touching on humans leaving the planet and inhabiting space. The vastness of space is obviously too enormous to ignore. So, you can be the judge of whether leaving the planet to help solve some of our environmental problems is part of the answer or not. Check out *Co-Evolution Quarterly*'s Space Colonies compilation of essays on this topic from the 1970s, edited by Stewart Brand. *Co-Evolution Quarterly* was a publication that influenced my views on abundant living in harmony with nature during that time period. There are plenty of opinions on this but I think it is worth considering in conjunction with Simple Abundance. An abundant life is possible on this splendid planet on which we live, and also possible in the abundant expanse of space beyond our atmosphere.

The abundance of space is easily recognized when gazing into the night sky. Venus and Mars are often visible, and with a small telescope, Jupiter and Saturn as well. If the night sky is dark enough in your neighborhood, The Milky Way is breathtaking. I remember learning that the Milky Way contains *billions* of stars rather than the mere millions of stars that I had thought. In fact, now astronomers estimate that there are <u>hundreds of billions</u> of stars in the Milky Way galaxy. This abundant number of stars is spread out in a spiral swath about 100,000 light years across.

Light years! A light year is that enormous distance that light travels in one year at around 670 million miles an hour. Do the math. Once again, the distances in space are beyond most people's ability to wrap their minds around. Earthly experience just doesn't give us the faculties for understanding the cosmos. One thing is certain: that the cosmos beyond Earth's atmosphere is unimaginably abundant.

Space just seems to just keep going on and on. In addition to the Milky Way, there are some 200 billion other galaxies in the physical Universe. Some, like the Andromeda Galaxy (the Milky Way's neighbor) is larger than ours and may have as many as one trillion stars. Giant galaxies, dwarf galaxies, and galactic clouds of every shape and size are all moving away from each other in space. Recent cosmological theories suggest that the Universe itself is vastly expanding. According to Stephen Hawking in his book, *A Brief History of Time*, the universe is expanding at the rate of 5-10% every billion years. This is based somewhat on the age of the universe being close to 14 billion years old after "The Big Bang". Hawking himself, along with Roger Penrose, is largely responsible for creating the mathematical proof that the Big Bang was, in fact the beginning of the universe in time. Considering that the nature of everything else in this universe is expansive, it should be no surprise that the universe itself would be also.

The Wilkinson microwave anisotrophy probe (WMAP) was launched into space in 2001 to measure radiation in outer space that was created by the Big Bang. The new data coming back from WMAP gives scientists a pretty clear picture of the origins of our universe and in fact, a date of the Big Bang – 13.7 billion years ago. There is also evidence that the universe came about during the Big Bang within a time period of just a fraction of second. All of the matter in the universe was created with an explosive force, beyond our scale of understanding, in a fraction of a second. The current astrophysical theory to explain how the universe came to be so large, and so instantaneously fast, is called *inflation*. Inflation shows mathematically how this is possible but the math is definitely beyond my reach. You can study this further by reviewing the work of Alan Guth, a professor at Massachusetts Institute of Technology (MIT), who developed the theory of inflation.

So, current cosmology states that all of the matter in the universe was created in the moment of the Big Bang. Then from a strictly physical standpoint, all of the matter that makes up the universe came from the same place. Yes that's right; every atom in every star and planet in every galaxy millions of light years from Earth all came from the same origin as the atoms that float through our human bodies that emerged from the Big Bang. Therefore, our human bodies are physically related to all matter in the universe; we are, in fact, made of stardust. It is not too far a stretch to conclude that our spirits too are connected to the Universal body of Spirit that contains all. The connection of matter, energy and Spirit at all levels of existence in the universe is one of the main topics of this book so we will revisit this idea frequently as we go along.

The universe is expanding and potentially new galaxies are forming all the time. But out of what would new galaxies be formed from? This is where the mysterious "dark matter" and "dark energy" come into the picture. Because dark matter cannot be seen or proven, the physicists today are all in a huff about what it is or isn't. But indeed, out there in the universe, beyond the immensely huge universe that we can see in night sky, there is something even <u>huger</u>. Evidence from WMAP tells us that the universe that we can see with our eyes and our earthly telescopes is only about 5% of the totality of the universe. All of the hundreds of billions of stars in the hundreds of billions of galaxies – trillions upon trillions of enormous burning suns – represent only 5% of what is "out there". In other words, about 95% of the universe is made up of energy and matter that we can't detect at all with our five senses. Michio Kaku, in his book *Parallel Worlds* describes dark matter as: "strange, undetermined substance... which has weight, surrounds the galaxies in a gigantic halo but is totally invisible. Dark matter is so pervasive and abundant that, in our own Milky Way galaxy, it outweighs all the stars by a factor of 10." (Kaku, p. 12). Thus, our vastly huge Milky Way is surrounded by an invisible cloud, many times larger than the galaxy itself that we can't see, but must be affecting us in some way. Even with our advanced 21st Century high-tech instruments we can't even detect about a quarter of the universe that consists of dark matter.

If gravitation were the only force affecting the universal bodies, then an expanding universe would be impossible – the universe should be collapsing in on itself. Some scientific research has led astrophysicists to speculate that dark energy creates an anti-gravity field that is pushing the galaxies outward to produce an expanding universe. Data coming from WMAP also suggests that the largest component of the universe by far is the mysterious force of *dark energy* which comprises over 70% of the universe. So, space is not so empty after all.

I don't know about you, but the more one looks into the true nature of the cosmos, the more mysterious and abundant it becomes. One could imagine that dark energy may someday be proven to be the actual creative energy of Source itself, who knows?

Years ago, I remember reading in a very prestigious science magazine that the source of new stars in our universe may be either: matter coming from a singularity in another dimension, or the result of matter going through a black hole backward in time. What did he just say? When scientists start talking about other dimensions and time travel, then that news really got my attention.

Talk of dimensions other than our three-dimensional world has always been the realm of occultists and science fiction writers. In the 19th Century, author H.D. Wells was fascinated by multiple dimensions and time travel years in advance of the revelations of Einstein and quantum theory. Now, mainstream science is deeply engrossed with the possibilities of other dimensions existing in space alongside our 3-D world (length, width, and height) and the 4th dimension of time. For decades physicists have tried to unify Einstein's theory of general relativity with quantum theory. General relativity deals with the immense scale of the universe, the Big Bang, space and time, whereas quantum theory is focused on the behavior of subatomic particles. Many physicists, mathematicians, and cosmologists are pouring energy into developing the current, most promising theory of all – string theory. We will revisit string theory in the next chapter when we look at the microscopic universe.

One of the most fascinating aspects of string theory which is especially relevant to cosmology is that the mathematics of the theory requires the existence of multiple dimensions. It wasn't long before cosmology was looking at the idea of multiple dimensions to help explain phenomena in the universe, such as: where does matter go when it disappears into a black hole? Also, theories about multiple dimensions might help to explain dark matter and dark energy. Ultimately, astrophysicists were led to develop the theory of multiple universes.

The multiple universe theory, sometimes called *multiverse* helps us to come to grips with a physical world that has all of these seemly impossible features. Just the idea of multiple physical universes is so far beyond most people's comfort range that just the mention of it will cause people's eyes to glaze over at a cocktail party. It's like our brains are just not wired to conceive the picture of what multi-dimensions or other universes would look like. A good explanation I've found for multiverses is the bubble model. If you can picture a bathtub filled with bubbles where the bubbles are connected to each other by their surface tension but are individuated bubbles by themselves. The bubbles change shape, become enlarged, they roll around, and they even divide and merge sometimes. But if you were inside of a bubble, you'd think that your whole universe was right there with you inside that bubble. The multiverse model that I prefer is the idea that there are an infinite number of universes that exist simultaneously with our own, but in different dimensions, thereby making them invisible to us. This idea of multiple universes coexisting side by side is often known as the "many worlds theory". This theory has particular appeal to those of us who believe in the existence of non-physical planes of consciousness.

The idea of multiple dimensions seems intuitively correct when taking into consideration all of the paranormal phenomena known to human kind such as: telekinesis, astral projection, ESP, ghost sightings, extraterrestrial sightings and contact, the tunnel and white light of near-death experiences; all seemingly just out of reach of our physical awareness. Any or all of these phenomena could be rationally explained as existing in a parallel dimension that momentarily interfaces with our three-dimensional world where human beings are operating.

Some physicists like the idea of multiple universes because it helps solve some of the paradoxes that result from quantum theory. We will revisit the quantum world in the next chapter. Even in basic three-dimensional thinking, our universe is immense. If the universe is infinitely expanding then the word *abundant* only scratches the surface of a vastness that is beyond our ability to even picture it. If there are multiple universes that exist alongside ours or enfolded in ours and only high level mathematicians and physicists can explain it, then our human imagination is probably the best tool to understand reality.

Here is why I believe that the physical universe is abundant:

- the Sun will bless our planet for at least another couple of billion years with abundant energy,
- our solar system contains several other interesting planets, a few dozen splendid moons, and millions of asteroids;
- the Milky Way Galaxy contains billions of stars, and an untold number of possible planets;
- our universe is infinite without any known boundary, and constantly expanding;
- new stars and galaxies are forming all the time from mysterious dark matter;
- things seem to move from dimension to dimension from an infinite number of possible universes, and
- time is non-linear and can possibly move forward or backward in some infinite fashion.

Like many of us here on Earth I've been fascinated by the stars and notions of space travel and life beyond our solar system. I don't comprehend all of the math formulas and theories that explain astrophysics, but understanding a little about cosmology gives me a great deal of confidence that the known universe is abundant. As for the unknown aspects of the universe, we'll have to stay tuned to string theory, M theory, and multiverse theory. My feeling is that the abundant nature of the universe will show itself to be even more abundant than we currently understand.

I know a lot of the far out science stuff just doesn't seem to make complete sense, especially coming from physicists who package their theories in complicated math. Oddly enough, we have to go even farther into the bizarre to get a better picture. In the next chapter, we are going to examine the abundant qualities of the sub-atomic world.

CHAPTER 3

The Abundant Universe – Quantum View

"Quantum Physics thus reveals a
basic oneness of the Universe"
Edwin Schrödinger

The world view is shifting quickly as the new ideas of quantum theory become more widely understood. Often though, a new idea may take many years to become part of a "world view", the collective view of reality accepted by a society. Science has pushed along our belief system in a series of scientific movements over the past 500 years or so. Scientific theories developed by Greek and Arab philosophers and mathematicians endured for many centuries and were the foundations of western scientific thought. Then, philosophers, Isaac Newton and René Descartes developed their theories about the nature of reality that didn't conflict too much with religious doctrine of that time - spiritual man and physical nature having separate existence and separate laws. That made Cartesian geometry and Newtonian physics easy for generations of people to accept. In the Cartesian/Newtonian world view, human beings and all elements in nature are separate from each other in a world that functions by certain laws that can be observed. The Cartesian rules of how the universe operates have become embedded in our societal institutions over the centuries. The adoption of these ideas into our world view explains much about what is generally accepted by society today: a world governed by the view that the various parts of the universe, especially our spiritual dimensions, are separate from each other.

This philosophy was based on a three-dimensional material world that was very real and measurable. Mathematics were developed that proved the laws of nature that were being observed and tested. Newton's Laws of Thermodynamics and calculus are still valid today for our understanding of many aspects of three dimensional nature.

However, around the turn of the 20th century, a group of scientists began developing a different understanding of nature through their observations of space, time and the subatomic world. Foremost among them was Albert Einstein, who linked notions about time and space in his theory of Special Relativity in 1904, and General Relativity in 1915. Einstein proved that both space and time were inseparable in a state that became known as "space-time". Only a handful of people in the 1910's really understood relativity but Einstein became an instant celebrity based on the brilliance of his theories. Relativity didn't replace the Newtonian physical laws but only added to the body of our understanding of the physical universe.

Taking further steps toward understanding the subatomic world were: Nils Bohr, Erwin Schrödinger, Paul Dirac, Louis De

Broglie, Wolfgang Pauli, Werner Heisenberg, and other physicists who spawned the field of quantum physics. Quantum theory explained certain subatomic behavior, and has gradually been accepted by the entire scientific community, even though some believe that the theory is not complete. Many everyday products today, including computers and cell phones, owe their existence to the discovery of quantum mechanics. Quantum theory, as well as Einstein's theories of general relativity and special relativity, is not fully understood by common people, and the theories are still not really part of the world view here in the 21st century. This is understandable because these theories shake the very foundation of humanity's beliefs about reality. Even though the word *quantum* has become a buzz word these days and the bookshelves are filled with quantum this and that, understanding quantum physics is tough. At best, a non-scientist type of guy like me can only grasp a small part of quantum mechanics, and it gets weirder as one delves deeper into the implications of the theory.

Quantum mechanics opened a can of worms when considered in relationship to the rest of our world view. How can subatomic particles, the "building blocks" of the universe, behave in a manner that is contrary to our notions about the nature of reality and not have an effect on our world view? How can we go on thinking that we live in a world of separateness when our scientists are telling us that we live in world where we are actually participating in creating the reality we see? How long did people keep thinking that the sun and stars revolved around the Earth after Nicolaus Copernicus, Galileo Galilei, and Johannes Kepler presented evidence that the Earth, in fact, revolved around the Sun? Perhaps common people continued to view the world as flat for quite a few years, but communication was slow then, and the powers of the church had tight control over information flow.

These days, communication is much more freely available, but change still comes slowly. One hundred years after Einstein presented the equations that integrated time and space as being relative to each other - the theories of relativity, most people probably still view time and space as being completely and totally separate. Relativity is a hard concept to wrap your mind around; quantum mechanics is even harder to understand. But understanding a little about quantum theory is necessary for a better understanding of the truly abundant nature of the universe.

My understanding of atomic structure goes back to grade school in the 1960's when every classroom had a model or a picture of an atom being an *object* with a cluster of protons and neutrons and little electron objects rotating around the nucleus. The model was great for our world view because the rotating electrons reminded us of little planets rotating around a big sun - another model in the classroom. Why of course the microscopic world of atoms behaves like our macro world planets and stars! As is often the case in elementary school education, the widely distributed visual aides are tightly controlled by various school boards and groups and thus the classroom materials are often decades behind the science. Our 1960s classroom had an atomic model circa 1900. The classroom model, of course, could never really portray atomic structure in the limited confines of a classroom of normal size. The actual physical size of an atom is more accurately described this way: picture the proton as being a grain of sand in the pulpit in the sanctuary of a large European cathedral like St. Marks in Rome, with electrons being represented by the reflection of a flashlight beam dancing on the inside surface of the cathedral's dome. Even though that atomic picture is rather arcane, it is the more current understanding of basic atomic structure. The vast majority of what we consider to be a *physical* particle called an atom is actually empty space between the subatomic parts. It is uncomfortable for people to think of atoms as consisting almost entirely of space because that's a very disconcerting thought: the ground you are standing on and the book you're holding is 99.9% space. What does that thought do to our ideas about what the world really is? What is this world made of? What is real?

To make matters worse, physicists have discovered that the electrons in the atomic structure behave sometimes as a particle (object), like our classroom model, and sometimes as a *wave*. Waves, of course, are not objects at all and behave quite differently. One of the most interesting characteristics of a wave is that they can exist in more than one place at time. An electron, when studied carefully, does not actually exist in a specific place in time and space, but exists in many places at once – an electron behaves like a wave. This characteristic of electrons was demonstrated in the *double slit experiment* (conducted by John Wheeler) where an electron is shot at a surface that has two slits and the electron actually passes through both slits. Only the probability that the electron will exist at a certain place and time can be predicted. The probabilities of electron behavior are backed up by mathematical formulas that make up the basis for quantum physics. Described as the *uncertainty principle*, this scientific thought says that nothing about the position of a subatomic particle can be precisely predicted - there is a level of uncertainty that is inherent in the behavior of the subatomic world. The universe is unpredictable which is in direct conflict with what Isaac Newton professed.

In the decades after the initial quantum revelations, many more subatomic particles have been discovered that go way beyond neutrons, protons and electrons. In the 1950s, 60s and 70s, with advanced methods of testing, a plethora of new particles were discovered within the subatomic structure of the atom itself. These little guys have names like W-bosons, Z-bosons, photons, neutrinos, positrons, muons, gluons, and of course, quarks. The name Quark has really caught on with people because it sounds cool. But for physicists the hunt continues for the subatomic particles and relationships that will unify the theories and the forces of the universe.

Most interesting to our understanding of quantum physics is that experiments (in particular, the *delayed choice experiment*) proved that the electrons would behave as waves until the moment of observation. But upon observation, the electron waves would "collapse" into the form of a particle (object). The human observer would help the subatomic electron move from the field of waves into our notion of reality called the physical world. The two slit experiment and delayed choice experiments demonstrate that the observer has an influence on the behavior of the electrons in the experiment. As Robert Nadeau and Menas Kafatos explain in *The Nonlocal Universe*: "The results of these (two slit experiments and delayed choice experiments) not only show that the observer and the observed system cannot be separate and distinct in space, they also reveal that this distinction does not exist in time. It is as if we caused something to happen after it has already occurred."

The founding fathers of quantum physics eventually came to believe that there were two different realities that were separated by a "wall" based on scale. One set of rules governs the physical laws of the universe, and they include Newton's laws of thermodynamics, and Einstein's relativity; these are the laws of the macro scale world. The microscopic world of subatomic particles is governed by quantum physics and the weird ideas such as the uncertainty principle and non-locality. These two sets of laws describing reality have been the guiding principles for scientists and others since the founding of quantum physics. Most high level physicists have never been happy with the idea that there are two different ways of viewing the universe based on scale and they have been trying for nearly one hundred years to unite the two different viewpoints with a theory that they are calling "unified theory" or, the "theory of everything". But until a theory is developed to unify everything, there remains a number of these paradoxes that physicists are grappling with.

I find it troubling that we can go on thinking that humans live in a physical world of separateness when, in fact, we can influence the actual atomic structure of matter itself. Can laboratory experiments be considered in a vacuum separate from human experience? Remember that experiments conducted on subatomic particles are very relevant to the rest of physical reality; subatomic particles are what the rest of the universe is made of. Can a physical object such as the chair I'm sitting in be considered as having certain laws of classical physics of Newton and Descartes but at the microscopic level of the chair's atomic structure, the laws change to quantum mechanics? Physicists have lived with this paradox for decades.

Science – Spirit Connection

In recent decades, the barn doors have been thrown open that used to separate science and spirituality. Some physicists are facing the paradoxes of quantum theory in unorthodox ways including embracing ancient spiritual philosophies that have a close resemblance to quantum physics. The connection between the Oneness of quantum theory and the Oneness of ancient spirituality is hard to ignore. It's no wonder that Fritjof Capra made all of those connections between modern physics and ancient philosophy in his ground-breaking book: *The Tao of Physics* in the 1970s. In the *Tao of Physics*, Capra showed that science and mysticism are not that far apart and he gave numerous examples comparing ancient eastern philosophies and modern quantum physics. I'm sure the ancients would agree too, because in ancient times, philosophers and scientists were one in the same. The science of quantum mechanics seems to be backing up the eastern philosophies of Hinduism, Buddhism, and Taoism. Capra writes that the eastern philosophies' picture of reality is "flowing and organic", and ever-changing. The idea of a changing, moving universe is a direct connection to our modern understanding of quantum physics. Ancient mystics often spoke of a universe that is in a state of constant change, as explained in the *I Ching* (book of Changes) written 2,500 years ago in China. In modern times, scientists are now saying the same thing. As Capra states: "The properties of subatomic particles can therefore only be understood in a dynamic context; in terms of movement, interaction and transformation." (Capra, p. 178). Because subatomic particles are in constant movement due to forces in the atomic structure, a real view of the material world has to include the dynamic behavior of matter – non-local electrons constantly spinning in rotational clouds of possibilities around a nucleus. Rotational behavior can be observed in our own solar system, and the other stars of the Milky Way Galaxy and, in fact, in the rotational movement of the galaxies themselves. Are physical objects like planets and stars really in a state of "possibility" rather than physical existence?

A new view of the universe has emerged in the past century that challenges the Newtonian and Cartesian models of the universe as being separate, static and predictable. By the early 1980's, many physicists were developing theories that showed the universe to be a place of wholeness, instead of separateness.

In 1980 physicist David Bohm began to explain the universe as place of connection and wholeness in his book *Wholeness and the Implicate Order*. Bohm believes that the universe is one enormous connected Oneness that we mistakenly view as consisting of numerous separate pieces. He describes the universe of connectedness as encompassing everything in the universe, including all matter, and all of space, as part of the *implicate order*. The implicate order is a field that encompasses everything in space and time. In this theory, even consciousness cannot be separated from the rest of existence, but can be considered a subtle energy force that interacts with everything else. Therefore, any notion of linear time must also be re-examined. Bohm uses the term *enfoldment* to describe how consciousness is woven into the fabric of the physical world, energy, and time.

Time

Everyone who owns a watch or a clock has a thought about time... probably numerous thoughts about time throughout the day. Like: "it's time to wake up", "I'm late to work", "time to go home", "time for dinner", etc. We measure time based on devices (clocks and calendars) that meter out chunks of "time" based on our society's agreement about what measurements are best for our way of life.

Most of our culture's ideas of time have to do with measurements of distance in space. For instance a year is the distance that the Earth travels in its circular orbit around the sun. A month is the time it takes the moon to circle the Earth. A day is the distance the

Earth travels to make a full circular rotation. These measurements of distance are all based on a relationship with relative objects in space: the sun, the moon, Earth. But the entire universe is in motion. Planets move around stars, stars spin around the center of their galaxies, galaxies revolve around each other in clusters, and everything in the universe seems to moving in an outward direction. We measure time against objects that we can see; therefore time is relative (just like Einstein said).

But what exactly is time? Time as a *thing*, indeed, does not exist. We have allowed ourselves to believe that time as displayed on a watch exists, when, in fact, it doesn't. Time, it seems, is a way for humans to trick ourselves into believing that events and things are separate from each other. Linear time allows us to view events as having happened in the past, the present or the future as if they were separate.

People in our culture have been intrigued with notions about time travel ever since H.G. Wells' 19th century book, *The Time Machine* and probably many years previous to that. But even with wild notions about going forward or backward in time, it was still considered to be linear set of events involving a "forward" motion and a "backward" motion. What if there were no forward or backward but that everything exists right "now"? It's pretty hard to picture. What if every possible past and every possible future in all the infinite possible variations existed right now? And what if human conscious could guide us through this field of infinite possibilities and interact with the field to bring into our physical reality certain aspects of the field? This is the model of the universe that I submit. Many physicists are working on proving this model with mathematics.

Experiments conducted by Alain Aspect in 1982, in France, brought new light to the notions about time and space, and the connections between "separate" subatomic particles. In this experiment at the University of Paris, two particles are separated by time and space but "communicate" with each other instantly (faster than the speed of light). The conclusion from these experiments is that there is a non-local nature to the fabric of reality. Particles are interconnected at some level so that they cannot be separated by any means of space and time. This characteristic behavior of subatomic particles is called *non-locality* and describes the behavior of particles that suggest the connection of all particles at some level. Everything in the universe is connected to everything else in a giant network. As difficult as this is to understand, try taking a flash light and shooting a beam of light into a prism of glass and see how the light actually appears to hit the floor in more than one place at the same time. Those light rays are part of the same thing, a *oneness* that has been differentiated by the glass prism, but a Oneness nonetheless; that is how light waves behave. So, could it be that everything in the universe behaves that way? Could it be that everything in the universe is, basically a light wave?

The giant network, or matrix, of the universe has become easier to understand with the development of holographic technology. Holography is a method of photographically recording objects with lasers which are able to be projected in a three-dimensional manner. The technology was pioneered in the 1960's and has been widely used in our culture in the past few decades. The popular 1980's movie, *Stars Wars*, featured a holographic image in the opening scene. Most of us are familiar with, at least the appearance of holograms, if not how they work. Scientists also have looked to holography as a model of how the universe works, as well. Such is the case with science when one new discovery leads to another and another, etc. Holography gives us a model of how the universe might really operate. Michael Talbot's book, *The Holographic Universe* exposed the general public to these ideas that some scientists, like Karl Pribram and David Bohm, had been working on since the 1970s. Neurophysiologist, Karl Pribram thinks that the holographic model helps to explain how the brain operates and physicist, Bohm believes also that holography describes the way sub-atomic particles behave as waves.

At the foundation of holographic technology is the concept of interference waves. Holographic images are created using laser generated light that is split into two beams, with one projected to bounce off an object, and then reflect back to "collide" with the original beam. The result is interference between the two different laser waves. This interference is then allowed to be recorded onto photographic film with the result being a holograph that can be projected into thin air to create a three-dimensional image of the original object. These three-dimensional holograms can be very realistic in appearance.

The most intriguing aspect of holography is that any part of the photographic image on the film itself contains the whole of the image. Unlike an ordinary strip of film that contains a single image that can be cut into many different pieces containing only parts of the image (a photo of a group of people can be cut into several pieces each containing only one person for example), holographic film can be cut into any number of pieces and each piece of the film contains the image in its entirety. This aspect of holography is similar to what mystics have been saying about reality for centuries: that each part contains the whole. Or as William Blake stated: "To see the world in a grain of sand, And a heaven in a wild flower, Hold infinity in the palm of your hands, and eternity in an hour" (*Auguries of Innocence*).

The idea of interference waves resonates with what physicists have been discovering at the subatomic level also. In quantum mechanics, electrons behave as waves until observed by the scientist at which time they behave as particles. Therefore, if electrons and other subatomic particles are intrinsically waves, then there is wave interference happening everywhere in the universe all at once. These interference patterns are what our eyes and brains interpret as being the physical world. We cannot "see" the wave patterns any more than we can see radio wave pattern interference in the atmosphere. For that matter, we cannot see the image recorded on holographic film as resembling the object that was filmed. Holographic film looks like a bunch of squiggly lines in the same fashion as stereogram pictures look, at first observation, to be an abstract pattern of colored blotches. When light passes through the holographic film, the image is created and we can make sense of it. And as we rest our eyes and mind on the stereogram image, the hidden image comes into recognition. It is our brain that creates the final image that our mind tells us is a rock, or a tree, or a familiar face. Our mind convinces us as to whether something is real or not. It's our mind that "sees".

The universe seems to be an enormous realm of waves that are interacting with each other and creating an infinitely complex system of interference patterns. Our brains interpret those interference patterns as objects or things that exist in the so-called "real world". And, in the observation of the interference patterns, we as observers help to bring these things into physical reality. We are, in fact, helping to **create** these objects. Human minds are creating rocks, trees, houses, the Earth itself! Humans are creating the stars and galaxies that we see in the sky at night. In the model I am describing, that is exactly what is happening. By observing the universe, a human mind is helping to create it. We are participating in creation.

Elements in nature respond to human intention at scales other at the subatomic level. In Japan, Dr. Masaru Emoto has conducted extensive research into the crystal formation of water, under different circumstances. Dr. Emoto's discoveries have lead to the conclusion that water responds to the thoughts and emotions that are directed toward it. For example, some water samples have prayers of peace and joy directed toward them, and some samples of water have messages of anger or hatred directed at them. The water samples are frozen and photographed, then analyzed. The crystals formed from water that had been associated with the positive messages of peace and joy had formed crystals that were well formed and beautiful – the classic hexagonal snowflake form. Crystals formed from the water samples that had negative messages of anger and hate formed distorted and malformed crystals. These experiments were repeated with many different samples of water and in different situations with the same results: human intention is projected into the crystalline structure of the water itself. Even experiments using written words (that carry emotional energy with them) produced the same results with words of negative messages producing malformed crystals and words such as *love* producing perfect six pointed crystals.

Physicists are constantly arguing with each other about theories. Some famous physicists seem to want to cling to a theory that they personally developed and then resist efforts to view the world any other way. Many scientists didn't want to move beyond Newtonian physics even though so many advances were being made in the 20th Century. Einstein didn't want to believe what Bohr was describing in quantum theory either. Bohr didn't want to hear what David Bohm was saying a little later in mid-century. Hawking broke new ground when he explained how black holes work but he was defensive when challenged by other physicists as to how to explain the total disappearance of matter into black holes. When the theory of multiple universes surfaced in the 1980s, the proponents including Alex Vilenkin, were attacked, or ignored, by their fellow scientists.

And now with string theory, physicists like Raphael Bousso are fighting an uphill battle against other physicists to forward a theory that challenges their long held beliefs. String theory though, has the potential to unite several other theories, such as dark matter, and multiple universes. The mathematics of string theory, and the more recent variation known as M-theory (membrane), requires the existence of more than the three dimensions of our current space reality. In fact, string theory requires at least 10 dimensions.

It could well be that string theory will ultimately unite the study of (physical) energy forces with the energy of the super conscious mind (non-physical). That is my hope, because the more physicists argue about the nature of reality, the more apparent it is that we are missing something important – we don't know the whole story. The universe _is_ multi-dimensional; we just don't experience the other dimensions on a day-to-day basis. But many people who have connected to the Source energy field at deep levels of consciousness, or who have had a "religious experience", or a "near-death experience", know that there exists realities other than what we see at the surface. Our world is filled with miracles and events that are beyond 3-D and beyond the five senses. See

Michael Talbot's book *The Holographic Universe* for numerous verified events in history that defy the laws of physics. Possibly, the energy that is experienced by psychics is related to the dark energy found in space. As we learned in the previous chapter, dark energy is pervasive in the universe, and may be the energy that is propelling the universe to expand. My contention is that science and society will come to understand the connection between the energy of sub-atomic particles, and the super-conscious energy that comes from Source. The abundance of this Universal energy, this energy that creates the universe, will become obvious to everyone.

If the super-conscious mind that we all have access to is also connected to an energy source such as dark energy, then we do, indeed, have access to the most powerful force in the universe. Someday soon, we can step into our true nature as creators along with Source. As mystics have always said: "we are One with God" (Source, Creater, Great Spirit). In essence, we <u>are</u> the energy that creates the universe.

Take a moment to consider the implications of an interactive Universe where we are shaping the very fabric of what we call reality. What does this tell us about the abundance that is all around us? Let that sink in a little before coming back down to earth in the next chapter.

Chapter 4

Our Small Blue Planet

"When you are in a hole, stop digging."
Bill McKibben

I've often wondered what it would be like if humans actually did manage to wipe ourselves off the Earth. Could we actually make ourselves extinct? If so, how long would it take for nature to reclaim the urban landscape? What species of tree would be the first to pop up through the cracks in the pavement? In eastern cities, it would probably be Alyanthus altisma, the so called tree of heaven that would be cracking streets and sidewalks from Boston to Atlanta. In my part of the country, Alnus rubra, western red alder, would be the first real tree to start splitting the pavement.

I've had the chance to see nature at work on abandoned human projects a few times here in the forests of the Pacific Northwest. There have been times when hiking in the forest that I've come across old railroad tracks in the middle of nowhere that date back to late 19th Century logging operations. Or, sometimes we can see ghost towns and camps where mining once flourished, and now the remnants of buildings, furniture and cooking utensils are all that's left behind.

It doesn't take long for the remains of human presence in nature to disappear. When a flood wiped out a bridge and a portion of paved forest road in the Cascade Mountains in 2001, two miles of the road were closed along with the campground that was at the end of the road. While backpacking in the area in 2005, it was easy to see the process of nature at work. Alder trees were sprouting in the asphalt pavement cracks and many species were taking root in the duff sitting directly on the pavement. In just 4 years, the campground was getting a little hard to recognize as a campground, without a discernible loop road and parking spaces, due to vegetation covering the man-made pavement. I felt a little like an archeologist walking through that campground viewing the moss covered picnic tables, rusty barbeques, and abandoned restroom building. It had been just four years.

Deep in the modern city, it may take thousands of years for most of the buildings to collapse but surely they would after a few seismic events, which are fairly common in geologic timeframes. Maybe it would take only a few hundred years. For a while it would be quite a sight to see 500 and 600 foot tall buildings popping up above a forest of trees of 100-200 feet height. In The *World Without Us*, Alan Weisman describes the way buildings in New York City would fail in a the city after humans were gone. Weisman describes the slow, natural way that water, both rainwater and groundwater, would cause rust and corrosion to weaken steel connections in buildings. Steel and concrete buildings, as permanent as they seem, are only as good as their foundations. The buildings would crumble and nature would pop up everywhere and most likely, wildlife would abound.

Many science-fiction books and movies have depicted this post-apocalyptic scenario so it's easy to picture.

The only reason for conjuring up images of a world without humans is the growing belief that people are damaging our environment to an extent that will eventually make the planet un-inhabitable for humans themselves someday; maybe soon. The extinction of the human race is now viewed as a possible outcome of our modern way of life. Humans seem willing, in fact eager, to overburden the planetary life support systems. Human population has almost tripled in the past 50 years from about 2.5 billion to 7 billion people with the result being a mounting strain on the planet. Resources that are vital for life, such as fresh water, and productive soil for farming, are decreasing at alarming rates due to humanity's practices of use, and abuse of the Earth. Deforestation and desertification are having widespread effects on the climate in parts of the world that may only be fully understood decades from now.

How can the world continue to produce increasing amounts of food for a population that is rising so rapidly? Describing population in his book, *Full House*, Lester Brown states that from 1950-1990 the world was adding about 50 million more people per year; now the rate is about 90 million more per year. The math of population growth is staggering: 90 million more people per year equals about 250,000 more people per day on our planet or about 10,000 more people per hour. If you live in a small town in the United States, by the time you sleep through the night and wake up in the morning, the human population of Earth will have increased by an equivalent of several of your town's population. Most of that population growth is happening in the countries where poverty is so huge, and health conditions are so poor, that they can least afford it. I can feel myself slipping into despair thinking about the enormous population numbers and the challenges they present.

For several months now, the grain ships have been arriving at the Port of Seattle to load up on wheat that is grown in the Palouse region of eastern Washington (one the breadbasket regions for wheat growing in the US). It's interesting to watch the ships from several different countries pulling up to the Terminal 86 grain elevator, just north of downtown Seattle. They unload grain from railroad cars into the grain elevator where about 4 million bushels of wheat can be stored. One at a time, the ships tie up to the dock, and a series of conveyors move the grain out in big hoses, and down into the hold of the ship. My guess is that most of that grain is making its way to India and China, where a third of the people on Earth live, and where their own grain harvests are not keeping pace with their population growth.

To keep pace with the growing human population, the world's food production will have to grow equally fast – 90 million more mouths to feed each year. Unfortunately, since the "green revolution" that increased crop volumes so significantly in the 1960's, crop production increases had already peaked by the mid 1980s. Increases in yields of rice and wheat, which really do feed the world, have slowed down measurably since 1990. Countries that used to produce an equal amount of grain to the amount they consumed are now net importers of grain, including China – the world's largest producer and consumer of grain. As China rapidly becomes an industrial giant, the good agricultural land and water are being sucked up and converted to use by factories that produce the clothing we wear and everybody's favorite smart phone. There is a pattern of declining agricultural production in proportion to the pace of industrial development in Asian countries. Japan,

South Korea and Taiwan have all had that exact experience over the past 40 years when their rapid industrialization resulted in declining production of grains (Brown, *Full House*).

The oceans, as sources of food for humanity are at the limit as well. The oceans are producing fish for consumption at capacity, or over capacity, throughout the world's seas. Any sizeable increase in harvest of fish stocks could cause a fishery to collapse as has happened at various times historically (which is why the fishing industry is so closely regulated). What that means for us is that there will be roughly the same amount of seafood available for an increasingly larger number of people – which of course results in higher prices. Personally, I'll simply cut down on my fish consumption, but for some of the world's people, they may lose this source of protein entirely. Of course, humans will find new species of seafood to eat that are a little lower down on the food chain – think shrimp, not salmon.

Most rangelands that are used for the production of meat animals have been maxed out and have very little possibility to be expanded, especially with the desertification that is on the rise world-wide. Water tables are being lowered in many parts of the world for the purposes of irrigation including a large part of the Great Plains states from Texas to the Dakotas that rely on the Oglalla Aquifer for much of their agricultural water needs. In Chapter 1, I loved writing about the flowing natural springs in places like Big Springs in Missouri, but it is depressing to think of the relentless pumping of that underground resource without adequate recharging of the aquifer.

Different, more sustainable agricultural techniques will surely be employed in the coming years. Raising crops on less land using less water may be the solution for us. I've seen some crops (strawberries and tomatoes) being raised in vertical tubes hanging from beams in a greenhouse where the exact quantities of water and nutrients can be added.

Possibly in the coming years, populations around the world could stabilize as they have in almost all of Europe and Japan. Twenty five countries, with a total population of about 700 million have stable populations with growth rates near zero. Of course, those nations are arguably the most advanced societies in the world and they are stable in many ways economically and socially as well. People may need to weigh their insistence on the "right" to have as many children as they wish with the "right" of future generations to live on a healthy planet. If people in the two hundred and thirty other countries really could understand what is at stake for their grandchildren, they would surely be making different choices today.

Recently, climate change has become the primary topic of concern among environmentalists. Most climate scientists believe that the effects of climate change will result in rising sea levels due to melting of polar ice caps and the melting of the vast ice cap in Greenland. The melting of Antarctic ice has been underway and documented by scientists for more than a decade. The melting of sea ice in the Arctic Ocean has some oceanographers believing that the northwest sea passage from Europe to Japan will actually be free enough of ice for summer passage in only a few years. Rising sea levels is a sobering thought considering that most of the world's population lives along the coastlines. This book cannot fully explore the huge consequences of climate change but there are many resources available, including the work of The Union of Concerned Scientists whose website is filled with articles by highly reputable scientists who have been studying climate change for years (www.ucsusa.org).

Humans have known for generations that overgrazing, overharvesting, and overfishing of oceans are recurring problems for humans. Ancient people and modern societies both seem incapable of stopping themselves from overusing a resource to the point of self-destruction. Today, extensive systems and practices encourage the best possible techniques in farming and there are strict fishing laws to ensure that that fisheries remain in a sustainable state. But, in place after place, the natural resources of land and ocean continue to be strained. Partly to blame are the economic and political systems that promote competition and separateness. Each individual, corporation or nation is out to get as much of a resource that it can for their interests. Individuals feel that they have to get their "share" before someone else takes it.

The world view which perceives all humans as "out for themselves" is an outgrowth of the economic principle of scarcity, and reinforced by systems of domination that have held humanity in this mode for at least five thousand years. Economic texts speak of "scarcity" as a state in which a resource is considered scarce when its availability is not enough to meet the demand. Our present western economic system is based on the resources of our planet being *scarce*. That concept is central to the economic system and thus is instrumental in the way we interact with the environment. On a scarce planet it is a race to control the scarce resources and exploit them.

Our economic system is an outgrowth of our world view of separateness. Scarcity plays into the idea of separateness quite well. In a world of separateness, we humans must think of ourselves first, above all other life. In fact, each individual human must think of themselves first, and foremost, to claim the scarce resources before someone else does. The ideas of scarcity and separateness dovetail nicely to justify and glorify the exploitation of the planet's resources, as well as other beings.

When viewing the impacts that humans have had on the planet, it is informative to view our human history of a few million years in the context of the entire lifetime of the planet: around 4 thousand million years. Four billion years of plate tectonics have made the planet unrecognizable from its former configuration. About 250 million years ago there was a single continent that we now call Pangaea that consisted of all of Asia, North and South America, Africa, Australia and Antarctica all combined into a single land mass. So, in just a couple of hundred million years, all of the continents have drifted apart like boats on a pond.

The human species has been around for a few million years, but the mainstream history of human beings is the story of Homo sapiens sapiens who have inhabited the Earth for around 50 thousand years. In that time period, people have spread throughout all of the continents on Earth. Humans have ingeniously made their homes everywhere from rainforests to deserts to arctic tundra and to most of the far flung islands of the Pacific Ocean. Unfortunately, the human story includes the narrative that is becoming all too familiar about habitat destruction, species extinction, and our human capacity for killing each other as well.

The record of human geography, and in particular, the growth of human civilization is not encouraging for someone who is trying to portray a vision of humans being capable of living in creative balance with all beings. However, by examining these aspects of human history and bringing to light the reality of **what is** will help to bring humans to a new understanding. It is emotionally agonizing to view the history of your species as plunderers, pillagers, and agents of genocide. But, we need to look at that history before moving on so that we, as a species can own it, and not deny it.

In the many thousands of years of "pre-history" we do not have a really good canvas for painting a picture of human existence. But with the help of archeologists we can follow Cro-Magnons into Europe and the Asian continent about 50,000 years ago. Of course those neighborhoods were already inhabited by the so-called Neanderthal humans who had been living at the edge of the great glaciers for about 100,000 years. As the archeological evidence suggest, the Cro-Magnons replaced the Neanderthals around this time. As these Cro-Magnon people replaced other peoples, their numbers increased and their hunting needs increased.

From about 50,000 - 15,000 years ago, Cro-Magnons migrated to every continent on the planet, hunting their way from place to place, probably in search of bigger animals or larger herds. Throughout the millennia, we can observe the pattern of species extinction that inevitably follows human expansion. The pattern is most obvious in the extinction of large "game" animals that surely supplied the early humans with food. In island environments, the extinction trail is the most obvious. Such was the case in Australia, where large marsupials and large flightless birds became extinct soon after the arrival of humans, about 50,000 years ago. The people who crossed the land mass between Siberia and Alaska 12,000 years or so ago were, most likely, looking for more food to eat, and they found it in the Americas. North and South America used to be home to many large game-like animals that are now extinct: camels, horses, mastodons, giant bison, and huge moose. As humans fanned out across the Americas, the extinctions followed.

By necessity, by accident, or by ingenuity, people developed the great new invention - agriculture about 10,000-5,000 years ago. Crafty humans started domesticating native wild plants and animals, thus creating a more permanent, stable source of food. The early agricultural developments took root in the Middle East, and in the Americas about 5-10,000 years ago. It seems that Native American hunter/gatherer societies adopted some agricultural practices and had possibly reached a stable population by that time. The present day hunter/gatherer tribes around the world do have a very balanced way of life that is in harmony with their habitat and stable populations, which suggests that lessons about ecological balance can be learned. Agriculture began the most significant shift in human history from hunter/gatherer, nomadic tribes to settled farming societies.

It seems very natural that the next development in human history would be the development of communities and cities - civilization. We will never know how the world would have evolved without agriculture, because the history of the ensuing several thousand years is the story of conquest and domination that has all but annihilated the hunter/gatherer cultures on every continent of the planet. We have, of course, very good archeological evidence of what came down as the result of the development of the early agricultural civilizations such as the Sumerians, Mesopotamians, Egyptians, and others. In case after case, we see the human's ever-expanding need to grow and develop causing environmental destruction and often the failure of the societies themselves (for more on this see Jerod Diamond's book *Collapse, Why Societies Choose to Fail*). The normal pattern of early agricultural civilizations was to develop unsustainable farming methods, overgraze and overuse some fragile soils with resultant erosion and floods to follow. Most often, the next action for a group was to move on to the next valley and start again, either on virgin plots of land, or displacing other tribes of people. To acquire new land for farming, military actions must have been more and more necessary - this is no doubt the origin of warfare and conquest. Standing armies were developed, and the ancient empires started to come into being. Not coincidently, this is the same era that spawned the idea of slavery. To put it bluntly, people conquered other people to take their land, enslave their people, and extend their dominance. As we will see later, the religions, particularly in the Middle East, changed to support the notion of dominance, during this time period. The religions themselves changed to justify the repugnant concepts of murder, rape and slavery.

Human beings have gone on for centuries, muddling through the process of evolution. Our track record is mixed: we have created arts of refined sophistication, and developed sciences to a fairly high level. In the process we have multiplied greatly and occupied most every corner of the globe with our farms, cities, and roads. Beautiful buildings and gardens grace the civilizations that we have created, particularly the monumental religious buildings such as: Angkor Wat in Cambodia, the temples of Timbuktu in Niger, and the classic Christian cathedrals of Europe. Juxtaposition the works of art that people have created in gratitude to God with the numerous wars, and it makes one wonder whether people are here on Earth to create beauty or cause destruction.

The impact of human civilization can be seen everywhere on the planet. But have human impacts really been significant in the larger perspective? Scale plays an important role in understanding how humans are impacting the Earth.

The environmental impacts that humans have made are no doubt significant. Clear-cutting of forests can be seen in satellite photos from space. Rain forest deforestation is taking place at the rate of several acres each minute, every minute of the day. Large strip mines have laid bare thousands of acres in parts of the United States. Rivers have been dammed, valleys flooded, forests converted to farmland, and farmland converted to shopping centers at a pace that never seems to slacken. These impacts are very real, and very significant from our vantage point.

The word significant comes up a lot when discussing environmental impacts. The standard for legally evaluating impacts to the environment in the United States is the Environmental Impact Statement (EIS). This type of document came out of the heady years in the 1970's that also birthed the Environmental Protection Agency, The Clean Water Act, and The Clean Air Act among others. These days, preparing an EIS for a major project is standard practice. The impacts, of say, a construction project are judged in an EIS as having *significant impacts* or *insignificant impacts* or *no impact*. Of course, whether an impact is significant, or not, is always judged from a human perspective; significance is a relative measurement.

What would constitute *significant* mountain building from the perspective of the forces that built the Himalayas? What would the word *significant* be in terms of plate tectonics? What would the significance be of building a road from the perspective of an ant or a beetle? We have no idea because we can only judge things from a human perspective of scale.

Because of our inability to really measure significance and because our culture doesn't want to limit economic growth, we developed another alternative to allow us to continue our growth activities, even though the impacts may be significant. Our culture developed the concept of *mitigation*. Mitigation is an ingenious way to let humans keep on doing what we want in terms of our economic expansion, but not feel guilty about it.

The Environmental Impact Statement (EIS) process and all of the environmental laws associated with our emerging environmental ethic are important steps in our evolution. However, as usual we have halted our exploration of environmental ethics at the level of laws, regulations, and enforcement. The human environmental ethic has stopped evolving; instead we concentrate our energy on refining the environmental laws that we have. We make up new ways to mitigate the impacts that we feel we are obligated to make for the sake of human progress. We recycle millions of tons of bottles without considering the options to the consumption of that many beverages. But we feel good about recycling! We haven't taken that next step to see what could be a better way of living. A Simply Abundant life awaits those who are willing to take a new look at our ethics.

In the meantime, an entire business sector has emerged that tweaks and re-tweaks the environmental laws. We have environmental engineers and planners, environmental lawyers, even environmental hygienists, and best of all, we have environmental marketing specialists, who can help reshape the way products are sold. Now we are led to believe from current marketing techniques, that we can consume our way out of environmental problems by buying "green" products that will make the world a better place.

Maybe by changing our consumptive habits somewhat by buying "green" products and recycling, we are moving incrementally toward a new ethic – it couldn't hurt. Building things out of recycled materials should certainly be part of any plan for life on a small planet. Green marketing is not inherently wrong but it does divert attention away from the real, much bigger questions. Businesses have an ongoing belief that humans can create these complex systems for living completely separate from the rest of planetary life.

By placing the human species in the context of all life on Earth, we can more accurately see what our impacts truly are. Human impacts can be evaluated using advanced systems of calculations including the method of calculating "ecological footprint". In the book by the same name, authors Mathis Wackernagel and William Rees (*Our Ecological Footprint*) analyzed the impacts that human activities have on the planet. Typically, impacts in this type of analyses are calculated by the number of acres of productive land that it takes to support one human living a certain lifestyle. In most of the industrialized western economies the ecological footprint is several times greater than the land area of that country. Currently, the lifestyle of the Dutch people requires 15 times the amount of land that is available for production in the Netherlands. Virtually all of the industrial countries have ecological footprint deficits. This deficit, of course, means that the populations of industrialized countries have to usurp resources from the rest of the world's countries to maintain the lifestyles to which they have become accustomed. A "quasi-parasitic relationship" is established between these developed nations and the undeveloped third world countries.

It is probably true that the affluent people in our society have a greater ecological footprint than the less wealthy, as was pointed out by Tim Kasser in his book, *The High Price of Materialism*, and wastefulness has accompanied affluence in the society we live in. The pattern is probably being repeated in the developing countries around the world because that is the behavior that the United States has modeled. In the growing economies of China and India, where 2 billion people live, it is commonly believed that environmental impacts will be widespread and impossible to mitigate. Total environmental destruction is inevitable if human beings continue to seek economic growth as the only goal. The expansion of negative effects from economic growth includes a breadth of factors that are only now becoming evident: loss of spirit among the world's unemployed young people; loss of indigenous cultures; loss of the voice of democracy as the false illusion of democratic institutions is revealed.

The growth based economies of Western Europe, North America and Japan are held up as models for the rest of the world. South American, Asian, and African countries are encouraged by the big global corporations, and the World Bank, to develop their economies using the same growth strategy models that have put us in the predicament that we're in. The World Bank loans money to these nations contingent on the funds being used for practices that are not sustainable such as development efforts in the Amazon basin. But, as ecological footprint analysis shows, the goal of all nations being able to reach the level of the American lifestyle is not even attainable using the current model of consumption. There simply is not enough productive land available on the planet; our "natural capital" is getting used up in a way in that is bankrupting us (to use terms that businessmen would understand). The business world is starting to catch on to the idea that our current path is not sustainable, which ultimately is bad for business, as you can imagine. In fact, the business world may be taking the lead in building a sustainable economy in the coming years, especially considering the failure of our political system to implement the necessary changes fast enough.

In Amy Larkin's book, *Environmental Debt, The Hidden Costs of a Changing Global Economy*, she gives many examples of business leaders who are actually leading the way toward sustainable business practices. McDonald's (of all businesses!) worked with Greenpeace (of all organizations!) to come to an agreement about how the rainforests of the Amazon are being affected by the fast food industry. The clearing of Amazonian rain forest for the purposes of food production is a classic example of how the carrying capacity of our planet is being pushed to the brink. On one hand, we need the rainforests to absorb carbon from the atmosphere to offset the huge volumes of carbon that our industrial world is putting into the atmosphere (climate scientists have that part clearly proven). But most of the Amazonian rainforest is in Brazil, Bolivia, Columbia, and Peru with a lesser extent in Ecuador, Venezuela, Guyana, and Suriname, which are all relatively poor countries (French Guiana is also a rain forest country but is part of France, which can't really be considered poor). Those countries, particularly Brazil, have allowed destructive practices in the Amazon to promote economic development of their country's natural resources. The main reason for rainforest clearing in Brazil is for the production of food crops, and cattle ranching, to feed the ever-expanding appetite of an ever-expanding population, who want an ever-expanding protein-rich diet. You can see how the growing human population and expanding economy are crashing up against the ability of our planet to support us

Expanding economic growth without factoring in externalities is an economic concept destined to create widespread misery along with the short-term benefits of growth. The number of externalities that are part of unsustainable growth are themselves growing in the current global market place. The word *externality* is a term used to describe an economic factor that is not immediately part of the business accounting equation, but is considered to be related externally. Externalities include environmental degradation due to economic growth activities which are not part of the direct costs of producing a product for market, therefore, not reflected in the price charged for the product. The cost of externalities, such as pollution cleanup, is historically paid for by the public, through taxes. Ironically, taxpayers who enjoy the low cost of the products then complain about the taxes without making the connection to the external costs of producing the product; there's a disconnect. Somehow, the connection between the citizens and government and business has to become transparent enough that people start to understand the true costs of our lifestyle choices. For example, the real cost of generating electricity by burning coal mined in Kentucky is heavily subsidized by the State of Kentucky itself (Larkin p. 139). Why not have state and federal dollars go into sustainable energy programs and create jobs like those in the booming solar and wind energy sectors? Government has, historically, had a huge role in funding for the development of major components of American infrastructure, including the aerospace industry, the interstate highway system, and the internet, just to name a few.

Business accounting can factor in externalities that will account for the loss of natural capital if they have a reason to do so, if it is in their interest to do so. Ray Anderson, founder of Interface, Inc. is one of the heroes of the business world, who is a model for business owners that are consciously creating a new ethic. Interface is the carpet manufacturing giant that was one of the companies that pioneered the concept of "biomimicry" in their products. Biomimicry is the process of learning from nature to find design solutions that work with the basic principles of nature, rather than against them. Interface has been committed to sustainable business practices for over 20 years.

Business investors, entrepreneurs, engineers, designers, inventors, architects, and builders have a lot to be excited about in the coming years as the world's economy is shifting toward different models. The opportunities to develop new business ideas are abundant just like the natural abundance of this universe – it just means taking a different look at things. Larkin gives excellent examples of innovation and biomimicry in *Environmental Debt*, but I'll just illustrate one. A Japanese transportation engineer was bothered about noise complaints from the super fast bullet trains that Japan's rail industry is famous for. This engineer was also a bird watcher, by the way. He was so inspired by the silent dive of a kingfisher bird as it dove into the water to catch fish that he redesigned the nose of the bullet train to mimic the kingfisher beak, resulting in a "new train that was not only quieter but also went 10 percent faster and used 15 percent less energy". (Larkin p. 177).

If a sustainable world economy is ever going to be possible, humans need to look at different solutions entirely. The abundant minds of people have no limit to creative solutions to problems as witnessed during centuries of human evolution. I have no time for people who say that the world must be limited because people have *always* been this way. We know from history that the world has been, and will continue to evolve, and spawn new ideas because we are tapped into Source, which is infinite. As with the business examples above, economists, scientists and philosophers are working together and moving toward solutions to the world's environmental crisis in new ways that are amazing. The Institute for Noetic Sciences (www.noetic.org), among other organizations, has brought together thinkers from many different scientific and spiritual disciplines to search for solutions that join science and spiritual thinking.

A Simply Abundant solution is in front of us, which will allow all people to enjoy lives of prosperity and freedom, if we are willing to model a different pattern of values, as we will see in the following chapters. But first, we have to dig a little deeper into base human behavior to see why we are in the environmental predicament that we are in to begin with.

CHAPTER 5

Planet of Separation

"There is something fundamentally wrong in treating the Earth as if it were a business in liquidation."
Herman Daly

For the past 5,000 years or so, our world societies have been guided by principles of separateness, wherein certain individuals and groups hold power over others. In various forms, people have exercised their power over others by extending the illusion of separateness, and then using that for conquest and empire building. In modern times, our world has been shaped by the concepts of separation, and our institutions reflect that. You might correctly surmise that the guiding principles of our modern cultures have been greed, aggression, and control. How did this happen?

The patterns of human modifications to natural environments, and dominance over other humans, can be traced back in an unbroken chain, from the early civilizations of the Fertile Crescent, to modern times. Time after time, in history, we see the path of environmental degradation, species extinction, and dominance over other humans as the pattern that follows us throughout the ages. The ongoing belief that humans are separate from the rest of creation, and even from each other, is the pervasive movement of the past several thousand years. This one idea has been the driving force that has motivated much of the philosophical, political and economic thought over the ages. The ancient connection to the Earth, to other species, and to each other, was most likely forgotten from an earlier time, or perhaps, was lost as the weight of competition and warfare overcame previous values in the human experience.

In modern times, the past few hundred years in particular, we have seen the human pursuit of economic expansion overtake all other values in importance. What happened to the other magnificent human values? Rooted deeply in the world cultures and religions are these things: a connection to nature; strong family ties; sense of community; and belief in God. Why have these values taken a back seat to economic expansion in the eyes of people today? We just seem to have forgotten. It is easy to see why values of connectedness to nature, community, family, and God have faded when pitted against the all-pervasive view that humans are distinctly separate and superior to all else. The American culture in particular glorifies the individual: the cowboy, the pioneer, the rags-to-riches billionaire, the superstar, and the superhero who does it all...alone.

To embrace a life that is simply full of abundance, one must know that the individual is a part of the Whole. Each individual soul is part of a collective Universal wholeness. Just like an ocean wave is an individual entity all its own in the collective body of the sea. The wave can call itself a separate wave for just an instant and then the ocean movement rolls on becoming other waves endlessly. People can call themselves individuals for an instant

(80-90 years or so), and then their bodies go back into the soil, and their spirits re-join the great Universal Source field, which contains all. Understanding the dual existence of individual and wholeness is an essential ingredient in helping to mend the human relationship to the planet, and each other.

Belief that we are essentially spiritual Beings, underneath the mantle of our bodies allows us to connect with all of the other humans on Earth. If one of us is a being at one with Universal Source, then we all must be. As parts of the same whole, it is a small step to see that we are all One with the Universe. In fact, each human individual *is* each other. I *is* you and you *is* me. Just like different fingers on the same hand - but in this case, the hand has 7 billion fingers. We are each part of a source of energy that is all-pervasive in the universe and we individuate as little conscious beings on this beautiful blue planet. Our consciousness is our Being, our connection to Universal Source. With that consciousness, we can expand our web of connections to all living beings on the planet and by extension we can expand our connection to ALL, period. All living organisms, the oceans, the air, the mountains, rocks and dust, are all part of the Universal Source, and are all part of us. More than mere "stewards" of the planet, humans are woven from the same Universal thread that the whole planet is made of. Indeed, we are part of the same cosmic material that the entire physical universe is made of.

Separateness

For many thousands of years our species lived in close communion with the abundance of nature and connectedness to the Earth as hunter/gatherers [author's note: there may have been several advanced civilizations that existed during this time period but it is not the purpose of this book to explore that possibility]. Then, gradually, between 5,000 and 10,000 years ago, humans stopped believing in connection and Oneness, and moved to the belief that we are all disconnected from each other, and the planet. Aboriginal cultures had an understanding of the abundant flow of Universal energy that seems to now be lost. The lost connection to nature was a gradual process that can be tracked by studying how humans acted toward each other, other species and their relation to Source.

As agriculture and grazing gained prominence during the late Neolithic period, abundance was still the norm for groups who were growing plentiful crops of grains and creating herds of goats, sheep and cattle. However, this abundance proved too much for the early civilizations of the Middle East, whose population exploded, and the degradation of their agricultural soils commenced. After building a prosperous agriculture society in the Neolithic age between 8000 - 4000 BCE, Mesopotamia had become a mess by 3000 BCE, with severely eroded soils, frequent floods, and famine. The great flood of Biblical fame that led Noah (or Gilgamesh) to build an ark to escape the rising waters was probably an historical account of Mesopotamian floods caused by overgrazing and abusive soil husbandry. Major disruptions to the early civilizations of the Middle East provoked a change in their philosophies. The religions of early civilizations started shifting about this time, as the people started looking to the gods for answers to their environmental problems.

For many centuries the early societies of the Middle East were guided by the feminine deities who represented fertility, plenty, and abundance. These early societies had rituals that honored the Earth for providing all that they needed. During times of abundance, there was plenty to be thankful for and the feminine gifts of abundance and fertility were honored with prayers, ceremonies, rituals, holidays, sacrifices, and feasts. These societies were generally peaceful, because with the abundance of nature at hand, there was little incentive for aggression. The earliest known civilization in the Mediterranean was on the island of Crete – the Minoan society, which had no standing army, no stockpiled weapons, and lived in peace in the Mediterranean basin for centuries.

But with the abundance of nature came a growing population that continued to deplete the rich alluvial soil, and exploit the more fragile soils on slopes for grazing. It was probably due to expanding flocks of livestock that initially encouraged people to start seizing the territory of neighboring groups. When fragile soil could no longer support the livestock herds of a community, the often preferred option was to attack a neighboring community and appropriate their land. Of course there would be counter-attacks which would necessitate the formation of standing armies for "defense".

In an arc across at least 4000 years of human civilization's history, the story is repeated over and over. Once aggression was in place as a preferred method of dealing with environmental or population problems, groups were regularly attacking and seizing the land of their neighbors. The cycle of arming for offense, and arming for defense, was impossible to stop. We don't have much on record of peaceful communities over the course of civilization's history because the peaceful societies were wiped out by their aggressive neighbors. If there were voices of reason at times, that were calling out for cooperation and consensus, their voices have been lost under a torrent of arrows, spears, bullets, and bombs. Or, equally likely, the reasonable people over time have ended up as slaves.

Slavery was another product of a policy of aggression and separateness. Slaves were an important source of energy for early civilizations, doing much of the physical labor in places such as Egypt, Greece and Rome. In Greece, during the time of the great democratic philosophizing of Plato and Socrates, the population of Athens was 2/3 slaves. Slavery continued for centuries with very little philosophical questioning by thoughtful religious or political leaders of any sort. But our history books are filled with the glory of aggressive societies: Greeks, Romans, Persians, Chinese, Japanese, and Mongolians.

In the early years of civilization, most societies had polytheist beliefs. A multitude of gods and goddesses were recognized, and honored for contributing collectively to creation. Civilizations eventually revised their philosophical beliefs to legitimatize their aggression. Feminine deities that evoked abundance and peace were lowered in the pantheon of the gods of the Middle Eastern societies (see *When God Was A Woman*, by Merlin Stone). Goddesses who were once honored as deities, were subsequently relegated to the role of wife, or consort, to a more powerful male god. Masculine gods who were equal or lower to feminine goddesses were elevated to more important roles in religion. Gods of war became common.

The religion of Judaism developed a philosophy of a single God almighty that replaced the pantheon of gods of previous polytheistic religions. A single almighty God could embody all of the notions of creation including peace and war; abundance and scarcity. He was, perhaps a God of neutrality for a time, not necessarily an aggressive God, until the political rationalization was developed to make Him so. The Hebrew tribes that eventually would become the people of Israel, came out of Egypt, into the Promised Land: Canaan. Canaan was, of course, not exactly uninhabited, so the Jews were encouraged by their leadership, as documented in the Torah/Old Testament Bible, to attack the people of Canaan, kill the men, women and children, destroy their towns, and take their land and their possessions. This strategy is clearly stated in Deuteronomy 2: *31 The Lord said to me, "See, I have begun to deliver Sihon and his country over to you. Now begin to conquer and possess his land."*

32 When Sihon and all his army came out to meet us in battle at Jahaz, 33 the Lord our God delivered him over to us and we struck him down, together with his sons and his whole army. 34 At that time we took all his towns and completely destroyed them—men, women and children. We left no survivors. 35 But the livestock and the plunder from the towns we had captured we carried off for ourselves. (Holy Bible International Edition).

This aggression is perfectly in alignment with the political aims of securing land for their population and the belief in scarcity. So deep is the belief in scarcity that the people of that time felt they needed to invent words from God that justified the murder, plunder, and slavery. There cannot have been a God in any people's religion that actually advocated what is stated in those scriptures. For example, there are dozens of Bible passages that refer to slavery and how to manage the business of slave ownership such as Leviticus 25:*44 As for your male and female slaves whom you may have: you may buy male and female slaves from among the nations that are around you. 45 You may also buy from among the strangers who sojourn with you and their clans that are with you, who have been born in your land, and they may be your property. 46 You may bequeath them to your sons after you to inherit as a possession forever. You may make slaves of them, but over your brothers the people of Israel you shall not rule, one over another ruthlessly.* (Holy Bible English Standard Version). Political leaders of societies used their visions of dominance to create and maintain aggressive societies based, in part, on these scriptures. More accurately, maybe, the scriptures were written specifically to justify the political agenda of aggression.

When the great struggle began between the polytheist societies and the monotheist societies, both religious philosophies had embraced the notion of God or "the gods" supporting and encouraging aggression. Ancient Greece and Rome, the Middle Ages in Europe, and then the formation of the American experience, represent a pattern of societies based on the same principles of separateness, aggression, and control, across twenty-five centuries. There are Asian examples that can be cited just as easily, but the Western European examples will be shown here because of the strong connection between the European cultures and their collective beliefs.

In ancient Rome, the Caesars held the vision for the establishment and maintenance of the Roman Empire for 500 years. The culture was based on an expanding empire, control of the people, and the hierarchical class system of empire. The energy of violence was "offensive" when the Roman legions marched off to conquer Gaul (France), Germania (Germany), or the Middle East. The energy was "defensive" when aggressive societies (Carthaginians, Goths) attacked Rome carrying forth their aggressive vision. Roman philosophy was still grappling with principals of science, and the politics of democracy, as were the Greeks. But the ideas were consistently based on separateness, and aggressive energy itself was instrumental in maintaining this culture of violence - there simply was no significant opposing vision of peace. Other than a few contrary voices, the system of control through aggression was the guiding vision of ancient Rome and most of the other cultures of that time.

Jesus of Nazareth brought forward a completely different vision for the world. His vision of peace and human connectedness was, of course a threat to the vision held by the powers of Rome and the elite class of Palestine (Israel) at that time. This little book you're holding can't possibly scratch the surface of what the teachings of Jesus held for humanity but we know that the core of his mission was for love, peace and connection to guide humans. Unfortunately, most of what Jesus taught has been lost in translation (literally) and the followers of Jesus, over the centuries, have often failed to carry forth his teaching. The vision initiated by Jesus was distorted by the actions of the Church leaders, who saw the opportunity to exercises control of their own over the population of Europeans in the Middle Ages. You might say that the vision of the leaders of the Christian Church for aggression and control over-rode the vision of peace initiated by Jesus of Nazareth. That's how the universe works: the Universe manifests the ideas put forth by people's thoughts and beliefs.

Even though Jesus spoke of peace, his followers became ever more aggressive. The early Christians, themselves victims of the Roman atrocities, quickly adopted the same or more cruel actions when Christianity overcame the polytheist religions of Europe. Millions of European women and men were killed (often burned alive) by Christian leaders to support their policy of intolerance of other belief systems.

With the gradual collapse of the Roman Empire, Europe organized itself into feudal kingdoms where land and resources were controlled by a ruling class of powerful thugs (kings, counts, dukes, barons, etc). The Christian Church participated in this organizational structure by establishing itself as a land baron who controlled vast areas of European land that eventually evolved into an empire itself: the Holy Roman Empire of the middle ages. The vision of separateness, aggression, and control, which was set up by the Romans across hundreds of years, was passed down into the feudal system. Aggression and land conquest were ideas held so strongly that they finally gave the impetus to organize the European continent into "nations". These nation states carried on the vision of separateness with the sharply divided social class system, political control, religious dogma, and standing armies for aggression and "defense".

Meanwhile, in the 7th Century, another monotheist culture emerged in the Middle East when Arab followers of Muhammad developed the religion of Islam. The spreading of Islam by the Arabs was rapid and aggressive. Islamic Arab armies swept across North Africa, throughout Spain, and as far as central France (Battle of Poitiers in 732). Cultures under Islamic rule flourished during this time and ushered in a new era of knowledge in the arts, sciences, and writing. Aggressive periods of conquest and subjugation were often followed by cultural advancement, which sometimes is given as justification for aggression.

While Islamic culture was flourishing in the Middle East, North Africa and Spain, Europe under Christian rule was languishing. Appreciation for the abundance of Europe's climate, forests, and soils, gave way to greedy attitudes of local land barons, who were constantly fighting for more of someone else's fiefdom. The "haves" and the "have-nots" defined the culture of the European middle ages, as wars raged among the ethnic groups for control and dominance. Beliefs in scarcity and separateness prevented much advancement of culture in general outside the walls of monasteries where knowledge was kept sequestered by the Church. Religious leaders encouraged concepts of separateness and intolerance of others and whipped up many crusades against people of different beliefs, primarily: Jews, Muslims, and Pagans.

The Crusades of the 11th and 12th Centuries and the Inquisition of the 12th to 14th Centuries stand out in history as two of the most poignant examples of political aggression and religious intolerance. The atrocities of the Christian's First, Second, and Third Crusades are legendary. Killing, raping, burning, and looting in the name of Christ were all part of wresting the holy land from the hands of Muslims. Whether any part of that would have been justified by Jesus is beyond imagination. Any notion of Christian, Muslims, and Jews living in an abundant world of harmony anywhere in the world was lost in the mayhem of that era. Ironically, it was in the Islamic capitals of culture such as Alexandria, Constantinople/Istanbul, and Cordoba that any level of tolerance was reached between the three main monotheistic religions groups. Under Islamic rule, Jewish and Christian communities thrived in those cities.

But living together in harmony was not on the agenda of the religious/political leaders of Europe in the 10th to 16th Century Europe. When the Crusades failed to secure the Middle East as part of Christendom, the Inquisition was unleashed in Europe to rid at least the European countries of non-Christians. Muslims, Jews, and Pagan people suffered enormously, and millions died at the hand of the Inquisitors. Once again, the notion of separateness was supported by religious doctrine; political agendas were backed up with an aggressive military action, when needed.

Around the same time as Christians were burning and looting their way to liberate the holy land, some cultures were experiencing limits to empire expansion in the American continents. Archeological evidence shows that the great Mayan civilization of Central America had exhausted their soils around the year 1000 CE. (Jerod Diamond, *Collapse*). The Mayans, too, turned to military strength to keep their empire intact. Encouraged by an elite class of priests, the Mayan empire continued to expand past the point at which that ecosystem could support itself. The large Mayan cities in Mexico's Yucatan peninsula, and in Central America, are testimony to how rapidly a civilization can disappear. It took only a few hundred years for incredibly grand Mayan cities to vanish into the subtropical forest. The cities are still there, of course, having been constructed largely of stone; the Mayan temples, streets and plazas remain to this day.

Unfortunately for them, keeping huge armies supplied on foreign expeditions was very taxing on a society such as the Mayan. Military adventures, in the short term at least, are very effective in enhancing life in the home society. Plentiful supplies of raw materials and slaves flow back to the capitals of the empire. However, as in the case of the Mayans, supporting huge occupying armies was extremely costly, and actually accelerated the decline of the empire.

There is considerable weight to the human geographical and technological influences that have shaped our cultures. As described by Jared Diamond in *Guns, Germs, and Steel*, those three factors in the title of the book, gave Europeans significant advantage over other world cultures, which allowed them to gain almost total control of the planet. However, most historians neglect or haven't imagined the influence of the dynamic Universal energy forces at work in our cultures. I think there is a direct link between the aggressive behavior of certain societies and the beliefs of the human beings living in those cultures. It is no accident that separateness and aggression became the cultural preferences; those were the visions of the people who were in the position of manifesting their visions. A brief look at United States history is meaningful.

By the time that the North and South American continents were being conquered by Europeans, the culture of separateness and aggression were deeply embedded in the societies of Europe. The policies of aggression were passed down from the Romans to the feudal lords, to the monarchies and Christian churches, and eventually, to the national governments of Europe. The nations of Spain and England were the most strident examples of aggression and world-wide empire building. North and South America are the direct result of that dynamic. By transference, those policies of aggression and domination became the mode for the colonies that eventually became the United States. Manifest Destiny, as the name implies, was a destiny that the leaders of that time were visualizing and manifesting through their actions. These men sat in their cities in New York, Pennsylvania, and Virginia and visualized a single nation that spread from the Atlantic Ocean to the Pacific Ocean. What a monumental vision - unlike anything envisioned before! This was the predominant cultural vision of the white Americans at the time. The destiny, of course, led ultimately to a policy of genocidal proportions against indigenous people of North America.

The American people were creating their visions based on a belief in separation and then bringing those visions into their reality through manifestation. Therefore the rationalization has been that aggression was a natural outgrowth of civilization's advancement.

For thousands of years slavery was a crucial component of the various economic systems that embraced it. Even capitalism and the American style democracy, which expounded the *freedom* of the individual, found a place for slavery in the United States into the mid-19th century. Private ownership of another human being was an accepted part of the world view and was supported by the Holy Bible! That world view shifted significantly over a period of around one hundred years, between the 1760s and the 1860s. Now, of course, we consider ownership of other human beings to be abhorrent. But to the average person in numerous past cultures, slavery was simply part of the economic system in place at the time. Slavery was referred to as a *"necessary* evil". This example shows how beliefs can dictate our behavior so strongly, and then eventually, how those beliefs can evolve and change.

This abbreviated history of civilization is intended to focus on the continuing theme of separateness that has permeated our modern way of life. The concept of separateness has worked its way into the religious doctrines, political sciences, and economic systems throughout history. The "rear-view mirror" view of this historical landscape shows us where our modern society now sits. And it is clear: we live in cultures that view individuals as being separate beings from each other, separate from nature, and separate from God. Notions of separateness show up at the individual level, and at national levels - nationalism itself promotes the idea that individual groups of people have loyalty above all else, to a fabricated institution of separateness – the nation.

The pendulum of history has swung in the direction of separateness for dozens of centuries, with horrific effects on human beings. Now, many of us feel the swing back toward the connectedness that our ancient ancestors had, and indigenous people have always had; we feel the energy of Source flowing through us, and pointing the way to where we once were, and where we are now going.

The only thing keeping humanity from taking the next evolutionary step is the limiting belief about the role we have to play in creating the reality that we live in. The world view that the universe is separate from us has been a foundation in western culture from the beginning of civilization 10 millennia ago. Eastern cultures have a different spiritual perspective but have more recently adopted most of the western world view, particularly in their economic practices. Every aspect of western civilization has separated humans from active participation in the direct process of creation.

We are taught about separateness from parents, school teachers, religious leaders, business owners, union leaders, etc. Our political systems are organized around separateness, as are our sporting events with their program of winners and losers. We have honored competitiveness to the point of absurdity. The concept of a superstar is testimony to western civilization's obsession with separateness. Being a star is not enough for our culture, we need *super*stars of entertainment and sports to really honor this fixation of our culture.

Even though an athlete is part of the joint organization of a team, a superstar athlete is given tremendous recognition and financial rewards for an ability that is only slightly more than an average athlete. For example a baseball player who has a batting average of .250 is considered average and would be awarded a modest salary. But a superstar baseball player with a batting average of, say .333 would be given a 10 million dollar salary, with advertising contracts, and other incentives, that may drive his yearly income up to 15 or 20 million dollars a year. A real-life baseball "superstar", Alex Rodriguez negotiated a salary just like this when he signed with the New York Yankees. No one doubts that Rodriquez has baseball talent that is a step above his counterparts. However, it is instrumental to view baseball statistics with a certain perspective: the salary differential between an average player who fails 3 out of 4 times (.250 batting average) and a superstar who fails only 2 out of 3 times (.333 batting average). All baseball hitters fail most of the time, with "superstars" failing slightly less than others.

Musicians experience a similar phenomenon with the recording industry. You hear a fantastic musician in a club and say: "wow, that guy was great, why aren't his CD's in every music store?" Then you hear a musician who is about equally talented, or less so, whose face appears on posters, on magazine covers, on talk shows, everywhere (Brittany Spears, for example). In our version of reality, we have a multitude of artists who are putting their work out into the world with little recognition and a small number of "stars", and an even smaller number of "superstars", who get the majority of recognition and money. A "nobody" is nobody until they land a big contract, and get that "golden ticket", that sets them up for life.

Our culture loves superstars. We adore celebrity movie stars, athletes, and musicians. The media sources fill pages and hours of discussion about what this celebrity is doing tonight or tomorrow. Our culture thrives on one person's triumphant rise to the very top of their professional status and then we watch in fascination as their lives are torn apart and exposed to the public at the grocery store checkout stand. Separateness breeds the competition that makes up our current world view. Why do we put so much cultural emphasis on a system that honors separateness? How can one artist be that much better than the next, particularly if they are woven of the same cosmic fabric? When viewed from a perspective of Oneness, our cultural trends look quite different.

What would a world look like if everyone won? What about sports where the athletes all work together to "win"? Can we imagine together a culture that honors wholeness with that same vigor that we currently honor separateness? Can we create such a world? John Lennon said yes to that question: *"imagine all the people, living life in peace..."*. What if all we had to do was *imagine*? What would the world look like if everyone just imagined peace? Or maybe just a percentage of the people could imagine a world where citizens of all nations, ethnic groups and tribes could live in peace on this beautiful planet. Living Simply Abundant is about imagining a different world, together.

Recent movements have given us a glimpse of the alternatives to the doctrine of the past that are available to us. The communication method introduced by Marshall Rosenberg called Non-Violent Communication shows us a new way to communicate. Cohousing communities show us a new model of how to live cooperatively, with social and personal connections being a primary tenet. Locally grown organic food that is sold at farmer's markets shows us an alternative to global factory food production. Local currencies are now in circulation, which show us that there are even alternatives to the biggest ruler of us all – money.

Simple Abundance can get human beings started down that path to interconnection with each other, and with Source. If we can imagine together, we can find out how powerful the energy of thoughts can be - thoughts are infinitely abundant and available to us in every moment. In the next chapter, we will take a look at abundance consciousness, and the law of attraction, and find out just how powerful we are in creating our reality.

CHAPTER 6

Abundance Consciousness

"What the mind can conceive, it can achieve"
Napoleon Hill

We are what we think.
Reality is a result of the thoughts that we hold.
Beauty is in the eye of the beholder.
Whatever I desire, I can acquire.
You can heal yourself.
Anything is possible...

It can be said many different ways, in many different settings, but the concept rings true for us based on our real life experiences – our thoughts create our reality. We've all had the experience of remembering something funny from the past, and when we bring that joke into the present, it makes us laugh. Bringing a joyful thought from the past and into your current thought stream has a way of immediately evoking joyful feelings in the present moment. Those feelings can be created in the mind based on past thoughts, current thoughts, or any thoughts, and delivered to the body in the sensation of feelings. Happiness stirs in the core of your body, and circulates up into your shoulders and head, and arms, and down to your legs; you might even lift yourself up imperceptibly, or tilt your body a certain way. Just the thought of something good makes us <u>feel</u> good. There is an obvious connection between what we think and what we feel.

Don't worry, be happy.

Happiness is what we want; sadness is what we don't want. Peace and love is what we want to experience, not hate and fear. Can people learn to create happiness in their lives by using their own thoughts, or is it a question of remembering what we once knew about living in an abundant world? There is good evidence that we already know this to be true, and we can get on with the easier task of <u>re-learning</u> abundant consciousness, and our ability to influence the actual experience of life.

<u>Ancient Unity</u>

This notion of an abundant Earth that provides plenty of sustenance to all beings is an ancient understanding that can be traced back to hunter-gatherer groups. These people enjoyed the abundance of animals and plants for food, and relocated as needed to stay close to those resources. Modern day remnants of hunter-gatherers in central Africa, Papua New Guinea, and groups in the Amazon basin of South America still enjoy a world of abundance. Anthropologists have postulated that hunter-gatherers are rich in their relationship to an abundant environment that provides their needs without worries of scarcity at all. Marshall Sahlins describes in *The Original Affluent Society* that hunter-gatherers typically work between 15-20 hours per week on food-procuring activities and daily chores. This schedule allows for an abundance of time for family connections, ceremonies, cultural events, relaxation, and leisurely activities. Oddly enough, this sort of lifestyle would accurately describe the freedom that a lot of modern Americans would aspire to.

The planet has all that we need to thrive; Earth has provided for the needs of people here.

Ancient people lived lives of togetherness in family and tribal units wherein the desires of individuals were secondary to the needs of the tribe or family. The success of the individual was the result of the success of the group. Tribes in ancient times had a connection to the Earth and honored the great mystery that created the abundant environment in which they lived. To this day, indigenous peoples around the world, including Native American tribes, have a very close relationship with the elements of nature, and all of creation. The Native American prayer that includes the words "all my relations", refers to all of the members of the community of creation, including humans, animals, plants, rocks, clouds, rain, air, etc. People who have this close relationship with nature often feel that their human community is *part* of nature, and they are participating in creation. Many anthropologists and archeologists now believe that people lived in relatively peaceful conditions as part of a greater Earth community for thousands of years.

The idea that people live in an interactive abundant universe has resurfaced in current times. Abundance consciousness has gained attention all over the world because people are trying to follow a way of living that will give them a sense of connection and lasting joy. The Law of Attraction states that whatever we focus our thoughts and energy on, is what then manifests as our reality. Thoughts = Experience. Our thoughts attract a reality that has a likeness to our thoughts. Therefore, if one has focused their thoughts on the good things in life, such as joy, and abundance, then that is exactly what he/she will experience. The inverse is true also: undesirable thoughts attract undesirable results into your life. The reality that we experience is shaped by our thoughts about it. We are, in fact, creating reality as we go along. Whether we want to believe it or not, the energy that is generated by our thoughts is bringing into our reality exactly that type of experience. Remember what we learned about "reality" from the previous chapters, particularly the quantum view of reality at the subatomic level? The universe is made up of vibrations; our brain interprets those vibrations, and creates impressions, images, and thoughts. Thoughts give meaning to the vibrations that reside in the Universal field; our thoughts are indeed creating the reality that we are experiencing. By thinking thoughts, and bringing the vibrations of that thought into our present moment reality, we then bring on the manifestation of that thought. The Law of Attraction is a law; it works whether we want it to or not. Therefore, when humans collectively focus on scarcity or lack, the energy of *scarce thought* brings that scarcity into their present reality.

The scarcity of resources, and lack of faith that the Earth will provide for them, probably drove early tribes of humans all those years ago to invade their neighbors, and enslave them. Thoughts of lack and scarcity are what brought on the 5000 year long era of aggression which created a vicious cycle of fear, attack, conquest, and then more fear of being attacked. It is the same pattern that is causing modern people to be unhappy and dissatisfied with their lives. The Universe is delivering exactly what they are focused on – the lack of what they really want in life.

Napoleon Hill's book *Think and Grow Rich* struck a chord with people from the 1940's onward. That book put forth the idea that holding strong thoughts and desires to be rich will make you rich. He was one of the first to expound on the idea that the universe was made up of energy that vibrates and is "filled with a form of universal power which adapts itself to the nature of the thoughts we hold in our minds; and influences us, in natural ways, to transmute our thoughts into their physical equivalent." (Hill p. 23). Unfortunately, most of us associate the word *rich* with money, which is, of course, only part of the story. The word has many other possibilities like: rich flavor, rich sense of humor, rich vocabulary, rich imagination, rich ideas, rich knowledge, or rich heart. The feeling that is evoked by abundance consciousness is one of sharing the richness of the universe, not just grabbing what we can. The overarching vision is about helping to create more of what we value and want out of life – it's about creation.

What about thoughts? How do thoughts help shape the Universe? The historical examples are many: inventors have always visualized their ideas before starting the experiments that would become life changing inventions. The Wright brothers had a *thought* about flying that eventually became an airplane that forever changed the way we live. Every architect has an idea about a building or a space that he wants to create before making drawings and building models. A chef's special dish, a piece of furniture, a fashion gown, tools, machines, computers, music, a space probe, a thimble, were all ideas first. It is fairly safe to say that every physical creation of humanity in this world started out as a thought, an idea, a vision. Consequently, people's thoughts are manifested through their ideas, and actions, and then these ideas become the physical world in front of us: buildings, cities, farms, etc.

Thoughts are entities in their own right, and ideas have power, even before they manifest in a physical sense. Thoughts reside in the non-material matrix of our universe, affecting the physical in subtle ways, such as the way an observer affects the behavior of subatomic particles in quantum physics experiments. When someone walks into a room of people carrying unpleasant thoughts of anger, frustration, fear, or whatever, we can usually feel that emotional energy and it affects us. When someone has a "bad vibe", most people can sense that, even if they don't know how it got there.

We humans are filling the universe with our thoughts in a manner that is similar to broadcasting radio waves into the atmosphere. Billions of humans are constantly transmitting a range of thoughts, from loving kindness to aggression. Each thought is an energy packet that contains information that affects the physical universe at the subatomic level. Each thought has intent and <u>potential</u> for manifestation. When large groups of thoughts collect in one place, they have a tendency to foster movements, social change, and revolutions - "revolution is in the air" as it is said. Revolution <u>is</u>, literally *in the air* - the thoughts and ideas are filling the non-physical matrix of the Universe, at a certain point in time. When thoughts are imbued with emotions, it gives the ideas even more power to manifest in the physical world. Emotions like love, connection, and sympathy, give birth to major movements of kindness, such as the outpouring of help that is given to victims of floods, hurricanes, and other disasters. At the other end of the spectrum are strong emotions such as fear, that foster racism, war, and genocide that have plagued humanity for millennia.

Because of the ability of thoughts to affect the physical environment, it can be said that thoughts are like seeds that contain the whole of the manifested reality. Every little acorn contains all of the potential of a mighty oak tree – the oak tree is enfolded in the acorn. The scientific model of the hologram is parallel to the acorn in that every fragment of a hologram contains the whole of that image.

There seems to be no limit to thought energy and the capability of humans to generate thoughts; it appears that thoughts are enormously abundant! It's awesome to ponder this limitless energy source of thoughts containing so much potential, as they are cast into the fertile soil of the physical universe; this Universal "soil" that seems so willing to manifest the thoughts of humans. It may be that all of creation (animals, plants, minerals) generates a similar subtle energy pattern. Work with Kirlian photography of plants, and psychic abilities of animals, would suggest that that is the case. See David R. Hawkins' book, *Power vs. Force* and other resources in the Bibliography at the end of this book for additional research on subtle energy.

So what is this non-physical matrix of the Universe, that feeds and nourishes thoughts, and eventually helps manifest the ideas into the physical form? The universe contains an unlimited field of energy. This energy field that makes up the universe holds the physical part of the universe in place like an electromagnetic field or gravity holds physical objects in place. Energy is limitless in the context of a universe that has no end.

To create the world that we know we want, we have to start thinking thoughts consistently about the world we want to create. It sounds simple enough, but there's lots of work involved. First, we have to make the decision to abandon the illusion of separation, and embrace a vision of a universe of wholeness.

Wholeness

To start viewing the world in a holistic manner requires a few steps, leaps actually. I believe that the world is ready for making some leaps of understanding and beliefs about the nature of our world, and the universe. I can see a world where humans, once again are members of a greater community of beings. We must consider ourselves co-existing with all beings, including animals and plants, and all members of the living, and non-living communities. I believe the day will come when we can view ownership of animals in the same light that we view ownership of humans today. If humans can see themselves as members of the Earth community, then visualizing joint ventures with other beings becomes easier to conceptualize. If we continue to see ourselves as separate from the rest of creation, we will not make the paradigm shift necessary for transformation. Anyone who spends time in nature has the opportunity to feel the connection with all other beings. If you allow yourself to feel the sun on your face or the wind through your hair, listen to the birds chatter, feel your feet on the ground, smell the seasonal smells of your place, you can indeed feel a connection to everything else.

Today, I am watching finches flying in frenzied action after a summer rain. They are landing on branches of the tree that I planted, picking things out of the roof gutter of my house. I shift my view in the window to get a better look, and the birds fly off, chasing each other. I realize that I am a participant in this bird action scenario: I built the house, planted the tree, and my actions in the window influenced their behavior. There is a type of agreement to that relationship. I can't help but feel like I am part of a community including my house, the birds, trees, rain, clouds, sky, and the Earth. For those moments of watching the finches flutter about, I had no sense of ownership, only feelings of connection. Once humans start to feel connected to other creatures, maybe one species at a time, then in a cascading series of connections, we will become one with the All of Creation. From that vantage point, we can look at how we participate in the act of creation itself through our consciousness.

Abundance consciousness is an act of participation in creation. With our intention, our thoughts, and our actions, we aid in the manifestation of our present reality. The universe can be viewed as a great big bowl of crazy ingredients, all mixed up into a hodgepodge. Imagine for a moment, a bowl of water, milk, oil, wheat flour, oatmeal, cornmeal, sugar, yeast, baking powder, salt, nuts, seeds, honey, etc. all sitting there in the bowl on your counter. Those ingredients have the *potential* of being a loaf of bread, cookies, brownies, pancakes, tortillas, and a whole host of other possibilities. With them all mixed together, it is hard to imagine a finished product with distinct features, but collectively, there is the "potentiality" of all of those things. What if you had the ability to selectively use just the ingredients for making oatmeal cookies and not the other ingredients? What if we could chose the cookies one day, and tortillas another day? What if our consciousness could act like the special chef in this scenario, and choose how it wants to consciously experience reality? This is the model of the universe that we are looking at now from the perspective of living Simply Abundant.

Universal Energy Flow

From Chapter 3 we saw that subatomic particles (the ingredients of our physical universe soup) behave like waves and can "be" in a variety of actual "places" in space. Subatomic particles are actually waves that are neither here nor there, until consciousness helps to collapse the wave pattern into a particle that appears in one place in our reality.

This model of the universe sheds light on the inherent abundant nature of the universe. The fabric of the universe is made up of energy (quanta, strings, etc) which changes form in a variety of ways. This energy has the potential to be any element from hydrogen to gold based on the number of electrons, neutrons and protons that are thus assembled. The flow of energy and physical matter cannot be destroyed, or made to go away; it all just changes forms, from solid form to liquid to gas, for example. The Universal energy rests in a latent mode until consciousness acts on it to create reality as we know it. In a sense, the universe is there, waiting for consciousness to cast its intention on it to create something. Universal energy is, of course, abundant, because it is the very fabric of which the universe is constructed - it is, simply, *all there is*. Universal energy is infinite. I use the term abundant and infinite almost interchangeably because when viewing the universe at this scale, it is infinite in every sense of the word.

The term "abundance consciousness" generally refers to the premise that people can use their consciousness to create abundance in their personal lives. This idea is in resonance with our understanding of how the Universal energy responds to human consciousness at the subatomic level. If the universe consists of energy that responds to the influence of human observation, (proven by the delayed choice experiment and double slit experiments, discussed in Chapter 3) it is therefore responsive, and thus, creative. This is true for individual consciousness, as well as the collective consciousness of groups.

Consciousness navigates through the grand recipe of potentialities of subatomic particles and assembles the reality that we chose to experience. An infinite variety of potential realities exist in the cosmic soup of Universal energy that we can choose from to create. They all remain in the state of potentiality until consciousness acts on them to manifest. All of the potential realities are as "real" as the next one; they just need to be brought into our present reality through manifestation. With the use of intention, thoughts, and actions, we are choosing the reality that we want to experience, and then bringing it into our present reality out of the gumbo of Universal energy. We do this individually, and collectively, as families, cultural groups, nations, etc. What we believe is true <u>is real</u> for us, and we bring that idea into our reality with our thoughts. The collective choices we make manifest in the political and social drama of our world which is based on our agreements about what is real. This drama is the outcome of our collective consciousness acting on the universal flow of energy to give us the reality that we are experiencing. Whether the reality that we see around us brings us great happiness, or whether it brings us despair, is the subject that we should be examining really carefully, since we all helped create it; this reality is what our collective consciousness intended. Our society could argue that point extensively, but if you are reading this book, you may be of the opinion that our present state of world affairs could use some change. We can implement that change through our individual and joint projection of our intention into the Universal flow of energy.

In every instant there exist an infinite number of choices that we are making - constantly. For the most part, we are making these choices unconsciously. We often make these choices based on our personal or cultural agreements that are set on automatic. Carefully analyzing choices about how we are creating our reality in every instant of our lives would be paralyzing and exhausting. We don't have to think to breathe because breathing is handled by our autonomic nervous system just like your heart beat, or cell division. However, we can use intention to set up a framework for creating our future that governs our choices, without having to make conscious decisions in every instant. Intention is the first step in creating the future that we desire. More on that in Chapter 8.

Time

We spend a lot of time worrying about "time". Do we have enough time for this or that. Am I spending my time well? Is what I'm doing a waste of my "time"? All of these thoughts try to quantify time in some way by relating time back to something that we can relate to. Of course our society relates time to money in many important ways such as salaries, paychecks, fees, etc. Some people go as far to say that "time equals money". The authors of *Your Money or Your Life*, Joe Dominguez and Vicki Robin refer to the relationship between time and money as "life energy". Each hour that you spend in efforts to earn money to buy stuff is exactly equal to one hour of your life's energy that is given up for the purchase of some <u>thing</u>. This is a useful way to examine how you spend your money, especially if you, like most people, work 40 hours per week, and receive a paycheck for your efforts. Each hour is worth only so much. In this perspective, your life's energy is limited to the number of hours you have left in your life. If you live, maybe 100 years then you have about 876,000 total hours in your lifetime. You spend, presumably the first 18 years at home or in school, then work, work, work at a job until you retire, say at the convenient age of 65. Therefore you have about 100,000 hours of time to "work". So each hour you spend "working" is, in a way, giving up an hour of your life for the purpose of earning money. This assumes, in a very simplistic manner, that you are primarily working for the sake of earning money to buy stuff (a house, insurance, food, toys, everything). This point of view sees time as a finite factor in everybody's life. How about viewing yourself as an infinite being who is having a human experience for awhile; then what is an hour, or a year? Nothing. Time is nothing.

As we examined previously, time as a thing doesn't really exist in the universe. Our notions about time are always related to the measurement of spacial relationships relative to each other. For example the time it takes for our planet Earth to pass through space around the sun is about 365 days, or one year. Time is all about the relationships between physical objects. Einstein said as much as he delineated his theory of general relativity and the concept of *space-time*. Time, space and physical objects are all bound up in our understanding of the universe and are inseparable. However, our culture's belief about time, space and the physical world, are viewed as separate, and therefore limit our ability to experience abundance. Time can be viewed as another dimension, and thus abundant, and infinite.

Our limiting belief is that there is only so much time in our day, week, or year. There is only so much time until I graduate, retire, or die. Of course dying is the ultimate limiting factor - there is only so much time in my life! What would your concept of time be if you believed that your true self was infinite and never "died"? This of course, is exactly what we are: each of us is an integral component of the Universal energy field that is infinite. Our soul doesn't even experience "time", it just *experiences*. Can people just experience the Now, and not view time as a limitation? Let's try.

Try for a moment, taking yourself off our planet into space somewhere, perhaps between our Sun and the next nearest star – Proxima Centauri, which is about 4 light years away. So, for a moment, put yourself about 2 light years out into space, several billion miles from Earth. Our beautiful bright Sun is just another dot in the cacophony of stars of the Milky Way galaxy in deep space. What would a year be? Well, if you wanted to think about it at all, a year is the distance that the tiny blue dot takes to make a circle around one of those little yellow spots, in the swirling tangle of billions other yellow dots. In other words, a year has practically no meaning in the space between our Sun and Proxima Centauri. A year has even *less* than no meaning if you imagined yourself out into really deep space, between the Milky Way galaxy and the Andromeda Galaxy, hundreds of thousands of light years away - more miles away than is worth trying to describe in this picture, in any case - really deep, deep space. Needless to say a month, week, day, hour, and minute, has no meaning whatsoever. What a person, or soul, would experience in deep space is a timelessness that is the true nature of the universe. If you could drop off a marker in space and then move in some direction, you could measure the distance from that object to where you are "later". But, that too, would be pointless, considering that you and the marker would both be moving in the same manner that everything in the universe is expanding in space-time. Everything is moving in the universe, so ultimately, it really is impossible to measure anything at all that is not relative to something else that is moving. That is what Einstein was getting at, by describing relativity to the public, in the early part of the last century. To this day, we are still having a hell of a time understanding it. Especially the part about what would happen to a person traveling at the speed of light in some direction in deep space, and how time would stand still for the human traveler; the second hand on his watch would stop turning, he would stop aging, etc.

We still cling to the belief that time is a real thing. Part of our trouble is that we are trying to use Earth "years" to describe something that is beyond time.

Humans are constantly using ideas from the past to describe things that are just beyond our understanding. Down through the ages, mystics have tried to explain the unknown – to tell us myths, stories, poems, koans, or other ways to explain things that we don't understand. The ancient texts were trying to explain the unknown to us in the language of their times. So, that is what today's teachers are trying to explain in the language of our times. The messages that we are getting from myriad teachers is the same thing: everything is connected to everything else; Oneness is what the Universe is all about.

The Law of Attraction is in accordance with the idea that consciousness creates our reality and explains it very personally – our thoughts create a vibration that attracts people and situations of a similar vibrational frequency. In the vibrationally oriented universe, like attracts like. Picture a tuning fork that strikes a certain vibrational tone of a musical note, say G. That vibration will activate other musical instruments in the room, like a guitar whose G string will start to vibrate and become audible; the guitar will start playing itself in sympathetic resonance. Music is a good analogy to Universal energy because the vibrations of musical notes are felt at many different levels. Other experiences in nature behave the same way. It is no great surprise that the atmosphere that surrounds us is filled with vibrations of all sorts. We have sound waves, radio waves, microwaves, cell phone waves, television waves, wireless internet, and more around us all day. These are waves that we can't see at all and we need devices to tune in. A radio tuner can help us tune into the frequency of a certain radio station that is broadcast at a specific frequency. We can dial up or down on the AM or FM dial to get the music or news that we want. Well, think about the human body acting like a radio receiver. Human beings can also "pick up" certain frequencies that are out there, unseen in the atmosphere. On the Universal field, all frequencies exist simultaneously and are available to us. When we hold thoughts on a certain frequency, thoughts of joy for example, the thoughts act like the tuner of a radio. Thinking joyful thoughts is like tapping the cosmic tuning fork for the note of joy on the Universal scale. At some point, the thought of joy will activate the other aspects of joy in the world, and those things will start to vibrate as well. That's the Law of Attraction at work – it already exists in the universe as witnessed by the vibration of musical notes. The leap for most people is to believe that their thoughts have the necessary energy to create the vibrations of real things in the field of all potentialities.

The latest understanding about the functions of human physiology reinforces what mystics have always said – the human body is both a broadcaster and receiver of information that exists in the form of waves. The wave frequencies are now being measured by instruments such as EEG and other medical devices. The body has measurable electromagnetic waves that are centered in the heart – the most electrically active organ in the body. This observation of electrical activity in the heart seems to confirm the cultural tradition which expounds that strong emotions such as love come from our heart.

The body has an electromagnetic field which can be measured and corresponds closely to the human auras that have been observed by psychics for many years. When the electromagnetic field is observed, the body glows in a way that seems to match up with the seven point chakra system. Electroencephlagraphy (EEG), and magnetoencephalography (MEG), technology let the electromagnetic energy be measured, and mapped by non-invasive techniques, from outside the body.

New research has found that the body is a receiver and conveyor of information through the pineal gland – the third eye. This gland that is buried deep in the brain has photo receptors that are designed to send and receive information over the airwaves, literally. Like the third eye, or sixth chakra, the pineal gland has been associated with psychic seeing and receiving beyond the physical realm to the Universal plane.

Recent science is coming back to what abundance consciousness teachers have always said: we are connected to everything, everything is connected to us, and infinite information is available to anyone. In the Universal field, all information exists in waveform throughout the universe in incredible abundance. Human beings have the ability to create thoughts that become our intentional reality by the graces of the Law of Attraction. Our bodies are sending and receiving electromagnetic waves of information that interacts with energy beyond our physical form in the Universal field. This relationship between the bioelectric activity of the human body and the energy existing in the Universal field is what creates the reality that we perceive.

We have the power to create our own abundant reality, but how do we, as a human society agree on what we want to create? How can we come to agreement on what reality should look like? Let's take a look at the common ground that exists between all of the individuals that make up the Oneness of humanity on this planet. Our commonality can unite all humans, and will allow us to advance in incredible ways.

Chapter 7

Our Common Values

> "Not Everything that can be counted counts, and
> not everything that counts can be counted."
> Albert Einstein

Human society is rich in diversity of cultures, languages and traditions; that's part of what makes people so remarkable among species on Earth. As diverse as we are though, there are commonalities in our desires and needs that illustrate to us our Oneness. The Oneness of all human beings is what binds us. Despite several millennia of separateness and fighting, now we have ever more reason to bring unity and Oneness to our world. As the problems from one country wash up on the shores of another, we see, more and more, that we are one people sharing a planet, and needing each other.

We are moving into a new era that recognizes where we've been, and we understand the choices that our cultures have made in the past to get us where we are today. Equipped with the knowledge that we have *chosen* scarcity and destruction in the past, and the wisdom that we can chose a different future, we are now moving toward creating what we actually want.

What do we want? What do we need to think about in order to create the experiences that we want, and what do modern people really want out of life? It is time to revisit basic human values. A new vision for our society could be for a society where there would be an abundance of love and time; a place where having time for connecting with family, friends, and community would be more important than having more belongings. This new society would be a place where *belonging* is more important than *belongings*. Abundance flows easily from, and to, a society of Beings who are connected to each other, and to Source.

In my conversations with liberal and conservative Americans, I've found that the desires for life are basically the same: we all want love, peace, joy, prosperity, and freedom to live our lives to the fullest. I love the part of the American Declaration of Independence that states that the Creator gave us the *right to pursue happiness* and that reads: "We hold these truths to be self-evident, that all men are created equal, that they are endowed by their Creator with certain unalienable Rights, that among these are Life Liberty and the pursuit of Happiness" [Declaration of Independence]. From culture to culture, and across the continents, people want the same essential facets of life that give them happiness. We want our families to be healthy, and our communities to prosper; we want to feel safe, and live without fear. These are universal desires of all humans, and that is exactly what the Universal energy field is ready to help us create!

The other day, I was listening to a program presented by the conservative think tank, The American Enterprise Institute, and listening intently as they described what everyone wants out of life – living in happiness. Their formula included, not surprisingly: faith, family, community, and work (specifically earned success from work). Deep down, people all want the same thing: happiness through the basics of human values. To get there, we need to cooperate with the Universe; we need to co-create the reality that we know we want with a source of energy that is prepared to deliver it. The belief in this principle is fundamental to creating a life of Simple Abundance.

For some reason, humans have needed constant reminders of the simple truth of our divine connection to Source. Great teachers have stepped forward over the years with the same basic message of Love, Peace, and Joy. The Middle East and India, in particular, have produced many teachers over the centuries, and the words of Universal Truth have spread slowly by word of mouth between cultures. Now the internet lets us reach each other more easily and gives us the opportunity to grow individually more rapidly. We can learn from others around the world and vast amounts of knowledge are spreading quickly. A bond is forming among people from many countries through internet connections that break down the barriers of culture and nationality. Teachings that originate in one country are discovered by others, and the words are quickly translated, and spread further. Many North American websites have English, French and Spanish options. European websites also include: German, Italian, Portuguese and often, many other languages. The book, *A Courses In Miracles,* can be found in twenty languages. In the past, language separated cultures from each other, resulting in xenophobia, but now language differences are but a small obstacle to the spreading of valuable spiritual teachings. The teaching of Ho'oponopono from the islands of Hawaii has spread around the world and now people in the United States, Canada, and several European countries are learning this beautiful and simple practice of prayer: *I love you; I'm sorry; please forgive me; thank you.*

The growth of human consciousness is palpable now. Groups of like-minded people are forming between many countries that are gradually breaking down the barriers of nationalism, and linking people into a deeper understanding of our connection to each other, and to Source. It is a great time to be alive and expanding our awareness into our world. We are, indeed, on a wave that is transforming our reality, and connecting us with our inner selves, each other, and the Source of all. How can we build on the momentum that we are experiencing now, and help create the kind of world that we would like to live, and prosper in?

First, consider that some things in this world can very easily be described as infinite or at least abundant. Love is infinite; it is the force that flows through everything, everywhere, and can be accessed at any time because it resides within us at a non-physical level. Feelings of love have certainly been felt by most people, and are universally desired by everyone. Romantic love is often held as our standard of what love is all about in this life, but there is more to Love at a deeper, spiritual level. Above all, love is the universal force that everyone on the planet feels connected to; it is our true nature. I like to call love the currency of the Universe; it is the mysterious energy that makes up, and holds together, the fabric of the Universal Source field.

The idea of Universal Love can be found in many cultures and religious traditions around the world. Despite their numerous historic differences, Christians, Hindus, Moslems, Buddhists, Jews, Taoists, and Pagans have spoken of love in its deeper sense in their scriptures. In a deep sense, I think we know that God is Love. The phrase: *God is Love*, was the essential message that Sathya Sai Baba brought to the world, and was repeated in all of the writings about his life.

We know of family love when we are gathered with our immediate or extended families, or when we think of them at a distance. The deep connection we have with our mothers and fathers, brothers and sisters, and children is one of the strongest bonds of love that exists. And we know of the love of friendships that sometimes span whole lifetimes and beyond. Love is desired by all of us, and it is here in its abundant splendor, as part of the natural inheritance of Beingness.

Peace is another abstract concept that is seldom experienced by people in modern society but is always there vibrationally below the level of our senses. Peace, like love, is a value that is desired by most everyone on the planet. We often associate peace with the lack of war, but it is so much more. The concept of peace is soothing to the mind, and conjures relaxed feelings of comfort, and pleasure. Peace also represents the lack of fear in one's life. There can be no peace when there is fear of any sort, as witnessed by those who live in constant fear of being attacked for reasons of ethnic tensions. Thoughts of a peaceful world bring smiles to people's faces and joy to our hearts. The abundance of peace in our world can be seen in the clouds in the sky or in the calm surface of a mountain lake. Peace can be experienced by anyone who sits quietly outdoors just being part of the community of life in nature – at One with all of Creation.

Joy in our hearts brings joy to the world. Joy is an infinite resource in our world. There is no view of past, present, or future that does not contain joy in some measure. Even the smallest flower growing out of a crack in the broken sidewalk in an urban slum can bring joy to someone. The un-stifled laughter of a child will bring joy to us, as long as there are children in the world. It is everywhere in nature and in our hearts; joy can be found, or created at any moment. Joy is infinite, and joy is accessible to everyone who can open their minds, and hearts a little, to let the flow of goodness come to them. Joy is one of the easiest feelings to create because all it takes is a thought and to share the thought takes only a smile. It's quite simple.

Love, Peace, and Joy are clearly infinite resources that are available to anyone on this planet and can be the basis of society's values if the people wish it to be. Abundance consciousness is based on the Universe being a place of infinite possibilities. The planet Earth is a small jewel of a world that 7 billion people share. If we made the infinite resources of Love, Peace and Joy the basis of our society, we would forever have those available to us – we would be living an abundant existence in paradise. We could live in love, and joyful peace, in abundance, forever, and never worry about using it up! Just imagine turning on a joy faucet, and letting it run and run. That *is* what we are capable of when we bring Simple Abundance into our lives and make Peace, Love, and Joy the priorities of the World; then, we can really live it up. What else do we humans really need to live happily ever after on our little blue planet? How do we go about living happily? We can just *live happily,* and then the Law of Attraction will bring more of it to us, and it keeps growing.

To enjoy the peace and love that is abundantly available to the people of Earth, we also need to live our lives in the absence of fear. We need to live in a *just* world, where we are free to pursue the highest good for ourselves, and for those around us. We cannot live in fear of our fellow humans and still experience the abundance that is our birthright. Freedom and justice must also be considered to be infinite in the context of this conversation, because of the innate limitlessness of these concepts. Freedom and justice are ideas important to human existence, but in essence, they are just ideas, and human minds have no limit to the extent that we can carry ideas forward. Ideas flow naturally from our minds into the Universal energy field, where they meet up with other thoughts and gain strength.

Tapping into the mind of humans and the Mind of the Universe may provide all of the answers we need. We owe our entire human environment, for better or for worse, to ideas that humans have come up with. Some people have cranked out ideas faster than the society had a chance to understand them; Benjamin Franklin and Nicola Tesla come to mind. We may not be able to develop our way out of the environmental crisis, but we can *think* our way out of it. It may seem like a cop-out to say that we can think our way out of our problems but, *think* again, we don't have any idea what ideas might come into, and out of our minds! That's the point: the mind is infinite.

What else do humans need in our lives, in the category of infinite resources, that we can safely create in our world, with total abandon, and not use up? Energy! Is energy infinite? Of course it is; at least in the context of the life of our Sun – about 6 billion more years of constantly radiating abundant energy out into space. Our little planet, third from the Sun, happens to be situated in space in just the right place to capture as much sunlight as we need to run everything for...pretty much forever. Plus, the universe is filled with billions of stars, each pouring out a near endless flow of light energy. Our universe is swimming in energy, and we just haven't developed the tools to access even a small fraction of it. What other kinds of energy exist in the universe? Nicola Tesla believed that there was an infinite source of energy built into the very structure of space around us; what I would call the Universal energy field. After contributing to the advancement of electrical power generation and transmission (he developed electrical alternating current – AC, which has made possible the electrification of the entire world), Tesla, at the time of his death, was working on a machine that would be able to draw energy directly from the field without needing to be connected to a major utility company. Needless to say, Tesla's funding was cut off by the major bankers and corporate leaders of the time (JP Morgan, Westinghouse) when he started to stray in the direction of providing means for ordinary citizens to have infinite, free energy. And as we saw in chapter 1, Mother Earth has abundant power to offer us, but the institutions of separateness are keeping that out of our reach.

By recognizing the abundance of the Earth, and the universe, and owning our abilities to manifest anything that our consciousness can dream up, we can live in total abundance and riches. Is our spiritual evolution leading us to live lives of alignment with Universal energy forces that enable us to manifest anything we desire out of the energy fabric of the universe? I think the answer is YES! Are we there yet? No. We may be hundreds, or possibly thousands of years away from the ability to manifest directly from Universal energy. But that's what clever gadgets will have to provide for us in the intervening years. Oh, and how we seem to love clever gadgets! There is no doubt that creative minds will have an infinite array of ideas to create gadgets for the future, maybe even Tesla's machine some day.

Obviously a world of full-on Creators would be a world inhabited only by responsible, highly-evolved beings. Otherwise, we would behave like the insane people who brought us the World Wars and all of the other wars on our planet. In that light, only a population of human beings who are in alignment with the greater intention of living in peace and harmony could be entrusted to a planet where manifesting all of our hearts desires was a daily practice. So abundance in a world of highly-evolved beings is the greatest vision for human evolution. We have many steps in that direction to follow before we reach that world. Our first steps include individual work, where we get in touch with our connection to all of creation, and our role in shaping our reality. Developing our ability to create is work that we can start as individuals and then come together as groups, and communities of people, to forge agreements about this great power source. Connecting with other species is the next logical step. As we practice manifesting in collaboration with other species, we will start to feel that connection to the creative energy source of the universe. We can manifest our visions, and be in alignment with other species, instead of the destructive course we have taken for several thousand years. Plants and animals have the same creative energy source flowing through them as we do, so it's visionary to imagine a world where communication and manifesting collaboration with plants and animals, can be possible. Instead of exploiters of the animal and plant kingdoms, we would be co-creators with them to provide what is needed, for all species.

Humans can work in the same manner with the energy of the mineral elements. As Dr. Emoto has shown through his work with water crystals, water molecules readily respond to the thought intentions put forth by humans. Just as alchemists changed the molecular structure of elements, people of the future will do the same thing with their intentions, and thought patterns. But the key to this process is manifesting only what is for the greatest good of your soul, and for the greater good of the universe (plants, animals, minerals, fellow humans). In other words, whatever you bring into existence through manifestation should be carefully considered to be beneficial for all of Creation.

When the new pattern is in place, people will be manifesting with the intention of creating a beautiful world, filled with an abundance of love, peace and joy. The natural consequence will be less negative impact on the planet and nature. People will be manifesting collectively in a vision where the interests of all human kind are considered jointly, along with all other citizen species, and elements.

Manifestation of human dreams is, of course what has been going on all along in our history anyway, right? Isn't that what civilization is all about? This is not a particularly new idea. Manifestation has been undertaken unconsciously by humans acting as individuals for thousands of years with no regard for the fact that we are creating our own reality as we go. That's what got us into so much trouble in the first place.

But we can create our future in the direction we want to go if we stay focused on the universal values that are important to all of us, such as: love, peace, joy, freedom, justice, health, and happiness in our lives, and in the lives of those on our planet. What makes Simple Abundance effective is that our intention is toward connection with everything else in a state of Oneness.

In the next chapter we will dive into the process of living Simply Abundant and understanding our nature as co-creators of the universe.

CHAPTER 8

A New Way of Life – Simple Abundance

"If the doors of perception were cleansed everything would appear to man as it is, Infinite."
William Blake

I've always dreamed that if I were ever given a chance to travel into space, and go see the moons of Saturn set behind the rings, I would go in a heartbeat. Who knows, one day we may be able to venture out into space, either physically or non-physically, to explore the cosmos, and contact other beings "out there". But for the moment, let's stay on Earth, and find ways to work things out right here at home. Today, our work is here.

The people of this planet are all part of the Oneness that includes the human species and all other species on Earth. Our connections to our fellow human beings are so strong that one can laugh at the differences that humans have held up as justifications for our separateness (DNA research is proving Oneness). We are indeed One. And we are connected to the source of creation in the universe that I have referred to as the Universal Source. The implications of this realization are enormous.

Humans, as co-creators of our reality, are partners with Universal Source in the creative process, which gives us the power to create the world we want. Every moment of every day, we are creating our own personal reality with our thoughts that shape our lives and experiences. The ways in which individuals use the power of creation is the topic of this chapter. The fashion in which our society collectively uses the Universal forces of creation will be discussed in detail in Chapter 10.

In the previous chapter we saw that people share a lot of common values that just about anyone can support. How do you feel about a world that is abundant, prosperous, free, joyful, healthy, loving, peaceful, and just?

We want the freedom to live our lives to the fullest extent, but we also have a consciousness about the state of Earth, our home. The two ideas are not mutually exclusive; we can live abundant lives that are gentle on the Earth. We can make choices that enhance our lives enormously and preserve the quality of existence on Earth at the same time. We live on an abundant planet, in orbit around an infinitely brilliant sun, in an interactive, abundant universe. How can we live the amazing, wonderful lives that we want to, and care for our gorgeous blue-green gem of a planet?

For starters, we can identify the parts of our reality that are easily identified as abundant; the "low lying" fruit that we saw in the last chapter. Love, peace, and joy are boundlessly abundant and infinitely available to us. There should be no doubt in anyone's mind that love has no limits. We can love every day, and the flow of love from the Universal supply is never depleted, it only increases, as it is shared among people and animals. Think of a pet dog waiting all day for its owner/friend to come home, and then lavishly loving every second of time with her; day-in and day-out. People do the same thing with little babies, and with their other loved ones. There are moments when your heart is filled with love, and you just feel like everything in the world is good and right. Feelings of peace and joy wash over one who experiences love often. Peace and love and joy are really the same thing because the three experiences come directly from Source. They are the three legs of existence in the abundant, co-creative Universe.

Emanating out of peace, love, and joy come a whole array of ideas, which also can be considered abundant, and without limits. Building from the three legs of abundance, we find more: happiness, contentment, compassion, sympathy, surprise, laughter, wonder, awe, curiosity, challenge, accomplishment, success, satisfaction, freedom, ease, and many more emotions of goodness. Why are these infinite? Because they are feelings; one can say that feelings are abundant, and infinite, right? OK, so how do we arrive at feelings? We choose them hundreds of times a day. In myriad ways, we choose between this, and that, as we move about in our daily lives, searching through the mystery of our reality for what feels right for us, our families, and communities. Sometimes we make some choices that lead us away from love, peace, and joy, toward things that we don't want, that are actually opposites of what we want. To learn more about choosing what you *do* want vs. choosing what you *don't* want, refer often to the book: *Ask and It Is Given* by Esther and Jerry Hicks (of Abraham fame), which has two dozen really good exercises that help us lead our thoughts back toward the feelings we want. According to Abraham, for every pleasing thing there is its unpleasing counterpart. It is up to us to focus on, and attract the things that are wanted, not unwanted. This is our work.

We want love, peace, joy, and all the other good stuff that is included in life on a healthy living planet. So many of those good feelings such as awe, wonder, peace, curiosity, challenge, and joy come directly from our experience of a living planet. I've stood in speechless awe numerous times upon crossing a ridge in the mountains to discover the valley below with snow capped mountains beyond. I've paddled a sea kayak into quiet bays where I could hear the breaths of a seal as he popped his head out of the water to check me out. Not to mention the breathtaking wonder one gets upon their first sight of the Grand Canyon from the south rim. Wow, awe is good. We take extravagant vacations to faraway places, looking for the excitement, and happiness we get from the beauty of nature.

Needless to say, we want a healthy planet that we can interact with. The time will come someday when we can communicate effectively with the other species that we share the planet with. We could certainly start that with dolphins and whales, whose fully developed brains and extensive languages are capable of... who knows what? They may have already been trying to talk to us for the past few thousand years but we just haven't been listening; we've been busy killing them. I can see a day when a Council of All Beings (see Joanna Macy's work) will involve humans, and many "create-tures" discussing the planetary issues, and the best ways for all Beings to live in harmony, and co-create together.

Of *course,* we want a healthy planet for our own sake, because breathing fresh air is so much nicer than breathing polluted air. There are a thousand other reasons that we want a healthy planet for our families and friends to flourish in. It seems that only during this current moment in human history that we've given the slightest thought to the ultimate future of our species, and the rest of life on Earth. But in that instant of time, the whole world view has changed. In my lifetime, I have witnessed the complete shift of people's view of our relationship to Earth. It was a watershed moment for humankind when those photos of Earth were taken from the moon on the first moon voyage in 1969. Anyone seeing that view of Earth must have felt something incredible but they didn't know what the photo was trying to tell us. Soon afterward, during the 1970s, the United States congress passed the Clean Water Act and the Clean Air Act, Earth Day celebrations began, the Environmental Movement commenced. People started to re-connect with the Earth on a deeper level and Mother Earth became *our* mother. There are many people of ancient traditions around the world who never lost their Earth connection, of course, but now modern urbanites are also feeling that connection to Earth, nature, our planet - Gaia. It is a remarkable transformation.

Simple Abundance is building on the foundation of what has already taken place in the last 50 years of reconnecting with nature. Most Americans are now familiar with sorting their waste products, and can soon start to call them "re-resources", instead of "waste". In my city, we separate re-resources into recyclables, compost and trash. We know recycling is helping reduce the waste stream, and raises the awareness of people to take further steps to live lighter on the land. It can be transformative too, if people take the Simple Abundance approach. Think about each element, be it metal, plastic, wood, paper, glass, as existing on Earth as a cohabitant of the planet. If every element is a brother or sister, then we should consider their well-being. Remember that every physical element is, in fact, a swirling vibrational wave interference pattern just like our physical bodies are. With a gentle thought, one can feel more connected to all of the things in the recycling bin. We can extend this thinking out to all kinds of practices such as: careful use of water, conserving energy and other resources, eating lower on the food chain, etc.

Practitioners of voluntary simplicity are already familiar with some of these principles. The idea that one's life can be simple *and* full is the best way to view voluntary simplicity. You don't have to feel that you are depriving yourself of the things you want in life because of their environmental cost – everything has an environmental impact of some sort. But in the Simply Abundant view of our life on Earth, we can have abundance through choices of how to live, and by co-creating with the Universe to continue creation infinitely. The Earth is abundant and will replenish itself with our co-creative practices. Ultimately, we have a major role in the concept of replenishment of nature but as we learn how to do that, we must walk lightly on the Earth.

In the greater view of the universe, everything is infinite – there may be an infinite number of universes! Until such time that people can understand their divine roles as co-creators of the physical universe itself, we will be living consciously and carefully on this beautiful globe orbiting our brilliant Sun. Reconciling this apparent dichotomy of living an abundant life on this small planet might be easier than you think. Human kind is constantly learning of the intricacies of creation, and our role in that creation; quantum physics is informing us of that. We are learning and evolving fairly quickly into Beings of higher knowledge and wisdom. The process of people consciously choosing the quality of our world will be the factor that saves this planet from human destructiveness. This is what might be called consciousness with a conscience. The time has come for us to consciously choose an abundant co-creative life for the planet.

Simple Abundance – Conscious Choice

Each time a choice presents itself in normal every day living, we can apply the filter of Simple Abundance. Depending on the scale of the choice, you might spend a second, a minute or several days, pondering the various trajectories that the choice could take. For example, if you consider buying a product that has a lot of packaging but you really want to eat what's inside, you can begin the "conscious choice" process. You could ask yourself some questions like these:

- Do you really *need* to eat what's inside?
- Is there another need of yours that is disguised as a desire to eat something?
- Was the product inside grown and harvested in a sustainable way?
- How were your fellow Beings treated during the process?
- Is the packaging able to be recycled?
- Is there a way to have the eating experience without all the packaging?
- Can this product be regenerated by nature easily?

You might come to the conclusion that this product is no good for you or the planet.

You might decide that you want it, but not badly enough, and will wait to buy it a different way that is less impactful on the Earth.

You might choose to consume the product, recycle the packaging, and then move on.

How can we shape and direct those choices to create the world that we want? We all share the common values of peace, love, and joy, and we want to live in a world where our families live in prosperous, healthy, and just communities. How do we do it? We create our new way of life both individually and collectively, because we are together in Oneness.

Every individual effort feeds into the Universal field and joins with all the uncountable number of other thoughts and actions in a matrix-like system of unimaginable complexity. The changes that happen in the field are sometimes hard to detect for years on end, as history has shown us. But sometimes things happen with striking speed, as witnessed by synchronicities and happenstance, that come into our lives increasingly as we become more aware. There is a scene from the movie *The Matrix* where Neo, the character played by Keanu Reeves, sees a cat twice and says to himself: "déjà-vu" and then, Morpheus, the Laurence Fishburne character, explains that déjà-vu events are what happen when the Matrix is being tampered with. As we co-create consciously, we too are tampering with the matrix/reality. When one becomes intimate with active consciously co-creating reality in the Universal Source field, déjà-vu situations pop up all the time.

Human beings, through our individual and collective consciousness, have created this setting that we live in. We have literally built this world from our imagination using our creative brains for generating ideas. These creative ideas and our flexible physical abilities, combine to create a human manifestation machine that has no limits. Each of us has seen amazing things in our lifetimes. But, we ain't seen nothin yet! The power of our intentional manifestation ability is largely untapped by humans at this point in time. The ability to dream of something creative and then build it in physical form is one of the first stages of manifestation. Many of the great inventors have "dreamed up" their inventions; actually seeing the invention in completion during night time dreaming. But we also see our acts of creation in every moment of the day. We, quite literally, create every moment with our thoughts. Sometimes the thoughts are unconscious, and sometimes, in the case of visualizations, the thoughts are very conscious.

We humans have the ability to adapt to a changing environment, generate new ideas, and create our own reality. The next stage for humans is to realize that everything already exists in this universe and our job is to help bring those things into our present reality. This is a powerful view of the Universe.

Creatively manifesting your own reality is something anyone can do, and that's why this work is so powerful, and ultimately why it will guide the world in a new direction. The influence of the media, powerful corporations, or the government does not affect the ability of common people to creatively manifest reality. It's possible that powerful forces throughout history, particularly organized religions have tried to suppress the knowledge that individuals can create reality; they have told us that only a select few have been chosen to interact with God, and you're not on the list. Individuals on their own can influence, impact, and create reality by themselves by working with the Universal energy of the universe – that is powerful knowledge that will change the world. Our job, our reason for being in this world at this time, is to use the Field for creation of a physical reality that is in harmony with our values of abundant love, peace, and joy with each other, and the other life forms on the planet.

We will combine ideas from various spiritual disciplines with concepts from social change movements to present the work of Simple Abundance. The goal of this work is to reiterate something that is already known deep in our souls - that we are Beings destined to create and now is the time for putting that into practice. The time is now, right Now. By reading this book, and accepting the principles of co-creation, we are already putting a positive vibration into the Universal field where the work is happening. Creating Simple Abundance is, of course – *simple*, and the more we practice it the stronger the results will be. Fortunately, we have a very powerful partner in this work; the Universe is, by nature, supportive of us, and wants to create with us that which we desire. Deciding what we desire is the key to begin the process of co-creating. The Law of Attraction states that whatever we focus our thoughts and energy on is what then manifests as our reality. So, where do we want to direct our thoughts?

There is a basic human belief that people should live in peace and harmony on Earth. We can extend that to living in peace and harmony with all of the living beings, and non-living elements on this planet. Springing from that premise, come our traditional hopes that our families can live in communities that are prosperous, healthy and just. I'm trying to paint a picture of utopia here because that is exactly what we should be aiming for. This new way of living is what the visionaries among us have wanted. A peaceful world is where Mahatma Gandhi, Martin Luther King, and John Lennon would all want to be; who knows, in another dimension they may join us, as John said: "...I hope somedaaaayyyy you will join us and the wooooorrrrld will live as one..." (John Lennon, *Imagine*). This way of living will create a place where all people can experience their full selves and potential. There will be abundant flow of prosperity to all corners of the planet. Children will grow up feeling good about themselves and supported by the world around them.

You may ask yourself if this is possible. There is a big "if" hanging over our world. If human-kind can manifest anything that they put their minds and thoughts to, why haven't we been creating utopia all along? Well that's simple; we've been busy doing other things. Sadly, our other work has been all about aggression, and by the Law of Attraction, what we've gotten is more of what we really didn't want: fear, violence, suffering, famine, war...the counterproductive stuff. That was people's previous work, up until now. Now, we have a better understanding of the Law of Attraction and how we have created this worldwide pattern of self-destruction. There is a fork in the road and one road leads toward further business as usual – aggressive separateness; the other road leads to peaceful connection with each other and Source. The choice is ours.

Choosing between one thing or another, plays a big part in the physical realm of life, but more so in the non-physical energy field. The Law of Attraction delivers what we chose, so we need to pick carefully. There are as many choices as there are possibilities – therefore, infinite. We are constantly choosing. When someone arrives at a decision point, they must make a choice between what is beneficial to them and the world, or that which does not serve the greater good. It is that simple...well, almost.

Simply Abundant Living– the Co-Creation Process

The basics of this process consist of the seven steps of Simple Abundance for bringing something from the Universal energy field into our current physical reality.

1. First is our **intention**;
2. next is creating the idea in **thought** form;
3. then the idea is **reinforced** by being spoken, written, or visualized;
4. then felt at the **emotional** level;
5. and experienced as **expectancy;**
6. then appreciated through **gratitude;** and
7. finally brought into physical form and experienced in our current reality as an **action.**

Intention, Thought, Reinforcement, Emotion, Expectation, Gratitude, and Action are the steps for creating a life that is Simply Abundant.

This concept is easier to acknowledge with the realization that all possible ideas, and all possible *things*, already exist in the Universal field of energy. All thoughts *are* things, as well, existing with energy, and vibrating at a frequency of their own in the field. Therefore, all things already exist in the field of Universal energy, and people make choices about what they want to think about, and do. It is all a matter of choice for people: whether to choose happiness or sadness, success or failure, peace or conflict, love or hate, and every possible choice in between that exists in the field. It's like being in a store, looking on the shelves of what to buy, and finding that the shelves are endless - infinite. Whatever we can imagine, we can create.

Our problem is that we have viewed ourselves as inherently fragmented and separate from each other. Until now, we haven't acknowledge our ability to co-create reality in partnership with each other, and the Universal energy that is omnipresent. People just a few centuries ago didn't think that electrical energy was of any use to humans either. They just thought of lightning bolts and static cling as mysteries they didn't understand and couldn't imagine being useful. People these days may wrongly think of Universal energy the same way, like the mysteries of the past - not really of any use to humans. However, Universal energy is infinitely useful and powerful; we just need to learn how to work with it.

Another way to see the Universal energy field is to think of the radio waves that exist in our atmosphere from AM and FM transmissions. The radio waves exist, but are invisible to human senses: we can't see them, feel them, hear them, smell them, or taste them. Radio waves just don't exist to the casual human observer, or their five senses; therefore, we don't think about them much. However, as a lot of kids discovered from building a home crystal radio kit, people can tap into this field of radio waves with simple technology - a crystal, antenna, and some wires. When I built my crystal radio as a young boy, it was way cool to hear radio station broadcasts coming through a little headphone, seemingly from the crystal itself. But the radio waves are there in our atmosphere all the time, and are invisible until they are received, and transmitted by the crystal. These days wireless technology has spread way beyond what the kid with a crystal radio kit could have imagined. Cellular telephones, Bluetooth technology, microwave transmissions, and other uses of the atmosphere are changing our way of life. Those technologies are mentioned here to open our minds to the way in which our thoughts are cast into the Universal field of energy on waves of a certain frequency. Our thoughts are waves.

In the present state of affairs on our planet, we have a lot to do to create the abundant reality that is our ultimate destiny, and to do that we will start with ourselves. Individual work is essential to creating reality at a larger scale in the world. Be mindful that your subconscious programs can block efforts to creating abundant reality in your life, or it can guide the creation process in a direction that benefits the ego, without incorporating the greater goal of universal wholeness. You see, individual success with abundance consciousness is useless without wholeness at the level of humans, other species, the planet, and the greater universe. Individuals who allow separation programs to control the creation process will ultimately disrupt the flow of Universal energy to everyone, because on the Universal plane, we are all connected. The success of one depends on the success of all, for ultimately, we are all ONE. The co-creative process can commence at any time; however, if you feel that your ego may have too much influence in your life, take some time to evaluate past programs that could interfere with your creative process and deal with that first.

Steps for Living Simply Abundant

The seven steps to Simple Abundance are: **Intention, Thoughts, Reinforcement, Emotions, Expectation, Gratitude, and Action.**

Intention

Everything starts with intention. It's been said that the universe is God's intention (or maybe it is *our* intention, as components of

Source energy). Everything comes into reality through the intention that is cast out into the fertile ground of the Universe. People are part of that creation process, deputized by Source to participate in the joy of creation. It is critical to start from the highest possible position of purity when generating the intentions in your life. Keep in mind that wholeness is the natural state of the universe, so aligning your intention with wholeness, or Oneness, is appropriate.

If we are intended to live in Oneness by the intention of Source, then our connection to our own intention is critically important. We have to trust that our intention is pure, and that we are worthy of our highest intentions for ourselves, and the world. Remember that if we don't truly believe that we are co-creators in this interactive Universe, then we are left feeling powerless, like victims of a fate that we have no control over. The co-creative Universe is quite the opposite - free will exists here that gives us the opportunity to create the intentions that we envision just like a sculptor shapes the clay of his work.

Our intention comes from a deep knowing that what we are intending is right for ourselves, and for the world. When we think about what we really want for the betterment of the world, it should invoke an elevated feeling of rightness for us. Our intention may have a passionate feeling to it and give us a thrill when we think about it. Our life's passion can be the guiding principle that leads us to clarify our intention for this lifetime. What is it that really generates passion in our lives? Does something generate feelings of excitement that well up inside of us every time we give thought to this idea? Our intention should be inspiring.

An easy way for me to clarify intention is to play the "what if" game. Here's how it goes: ask yourself a simple question about any situation that you can imagine as you may want it to be, or are just curious about what it would be like if it were actually happening. Arriving at intention can be the result of asking broad, wide-open questions like: "what if everyone on Earth wanted peace and believed that is was possible?" Let yourself just fantasize for a few minutes on what that world would look like in your mind's eye. Personally, this particular "what if" thought gives me great joy to think about, because the images that come to mind are always filled with grace and optimism for peace on Earth. This train of thought could lead one to decide that world peace was the intention that fits them most closely. Or, you could play "what if" on a more personal level, like: "what if I were able to talk to animals and hear what they had to say about life on Earth?" Let your imagination run wild with "what if" questions that don't have to be grounded in any kind of present day reality – the sky's the limit with this fun exercise (imagine having breakfast with your favorite animal and discussing current events). You don't want to limit yourself, because limitations are for the un-empowered, and we're powerful co-creators living our intentions in Simple Abundance.

So, here are a few guidelines for connecting to your intentions:

- Allow the intention to flow from your highest self that is a co-creator of this Universe of fantastic creation.
- Access the most vaunted, high-minded ideas, and your deepest core values about the goodness in the world.
- Be wide open to the infinite possibilities of creation and don't be limited by what you think the present reality looks like.
- Have fun with it.
- Let your passion and inspirations guide you.

Thoughts

Thoughts are energy forms that are a part of us, and part of the field of energy that permeates the universe. Just like any form of energy, thoughts can change form, but cannot be destroyed. The first Law of Thermodynamics and the principle of the Conservation of Energy state that energy cannot be created nor destroyed, but can only change form. Thus, thoughts exist for eternity in our universe. They are little packets of energy that interact with the Universal energy field in much the same way as radio signals are broadcast on the electromagnetic field. Thought energy is broadcast at frequencies that we cannot detect with current technology. However, science is getting closer to discovering ways to measure this subtle energy, in much the same way that dark energy is being studied by cosmologists.

Thoughts, once cast into the Universal energy field, react with the other creative forces of the universe to create interference waves in a manner similar to interference waves in an electromagnetic field. A good analogy is that, if you dropped a pebble into a pool of still water, you would create a series of little ripples that emanate from the point on the pool that the pebble hit the water. If you cast another pebble into the water in a different place, the waves from the new ripples would collide with the waves from the original pebble, thus creating interference waves that look like a combination of the two ripples. The more pebbles that are thrown into the water, the more complex the interference pattern starts to look. The ripples created on the water surface are individual and separate from each other for the moment, and when the ripples collide at some point, they create an interference pattern that is different from either of the two individual wave patterns. Imagine thoughts as being little pebbles being cast into the still pond of the Universal energy field.

Understandably, it is a great leap of faith to go from the understanding that the universe is made up of untold trillions of tiny little objects called atoms, to the notion that those atoms aren't really *objects* at all but, in fact, just plain energy. Renowned Austrian quantum physicist, Erwin Schrödinger said: "What we observe as material bodies and forces are nothing but shapes and variations in the structure of space". If you can wrap your mind part way around this idea, it is a good start to becoming a co-creator with Simple Abundance. I suggest reading as much as possible about what physicists are telling us about the nature of the universe. The book *The Field* by Lynn McTaggert consolidates a lot of data, gives clear explanations of scientific discoveries, and presents examples of ways that people's energy interacts with the Universe in creative ways. Brian Greene, author of *The Elegant Universe* is a physicist, who also has some stage presence, stars in a number of videos on the internet, and has had many television shows produced, including several episodes of the excellent scientific show, *Nova*. Greene has an excellent ability to explain complex scientific principles in an understandable, and entertaining, way.

The next leap of faith is a big one, also. Try to view your thoughts as little packets of energy that interact in the universe just like the packets of energy that we call electrons or photons. Just as a photon is a packet of light energy that you cannot see, until you see it hit an object. We see this every day, when the light from the sun hits our planet, all day long. As the light photons land on earthly objects, it is the *reflection* of the light that we actually "see", and that gives us all that we observe on Earth. It is the same with thoughts – they are invisible little packets of energy that are cast out every day into the universe, and we are not aware of them until we see the reflection of the thought manifested in our world. Just as the photons of light bounce off a flower and give us a brilliant color, thoughts bounce off other energy waves to create what we perceive as our reality. What we experience in our daily lives is a *reflection* of our thoughts. Good thoughts, bad thoughts, they all bounce back to us in this interactive energy field.

These thought fields interact with the other information in the universe, such as electromagnetic fields to create the experiences we have everywhere in our world. They are the fabric of our worldly belief systems. This is to say, that the thought fields are created by us collectively, and our cultures, and societies are based on the content of those fields. The ripple effect of billions of people putting out billions of thoughts a day are merging in the field of Universal energy and creating the world as we know it. The world is an extremely complex place! That's because there are so many thoughts being cast into the field at the same time. Some thoughts are in direct conflict with each other and have a tendency to negate each other; we see that in politics all of the time. When energy waves of different frequencies collide they may create *destructive interference* and cancel each other out. When two waves of equal or similar frequencies interact with each other in a field, they form a coherent pattern called *constructive interference*.

Imagine if thoughts from many, many people were cast into the universe along the same frequency, such as the energy of peace, to form constructive interference patterns in the Universal energy field. The frequency of peace can be felt by ordinary people at many different levels. Have you ever walked into a gathering of people who all had a thought of love in their minds? We have probably all felt the peace of a place when a spiritual event is happening at a church, temple, or in the company of a group of monks, or some like-minded people. We might say something like: "it sure feels peaceful here". What we are feeling is the resonance of many, many, many thoughts being cast into the Universal field. Thoughts are waves just like sound waves but with more subtle characteristics. Chanting of bhajans, in the Hindu devotional music tradition, is a good example of how powerful the resonance of sound waves can be, especially when combined with the spiritual force of the thoughts that go along with the chants.

Positive energy fields are created when positive, loving, or healing thoughts are projected into the Universal field. The loving atmosphere can be clearly sensed by the average person. We don't have a way of measuring it because the feeling that we get from a loving field of energy is not sensed by our hearing, seeing, smelling, tasting, or touching senses. But it is still very real and present. I've had experiences when I was in India many years ago, in the ashram of Satya Sai Baba, where thousands of people were gathered to see Baba. Most days, Baba would walk among the people in the courtyard, or give darshan (the sharing of time between a holy person and his devotees) in the assembly hall. The amazing thing, though, was that the energy level was very high, even before Baba entered the room, or the courtyard where he gave darshan most days. The people, the devotees, in their expectations of Baba's presence, were creating an energy field with their thoughts that was filling the space, and creating a powerful field of love that was clearly perceptible to all. I am sure that many Indian people, Europeans, Americans, and others came to Baba's ashram to experience this field of love which they associated with the presence of Baba but was, in fact, generated by the thousands of people themselves. These feelings of love were the basis for Sai Baba's teaching. Baba would say: "Start the day with love, fill the day with love, and end the day with love".

Undoubtedly, that field of love generated by people's thoughts was Baba's intention all along.

Positive energy fields can be found in the presence of leaders who have high ideals and teachings. Huge fields of peaceful vibrations must have surrounded people like Mahatma Gandhi, Jesus of Nazareth, Mohamed, the Buddha, and St. Francis of Assisi. In my lifetime, the peaceful, loving field of energy could be found in the presence of Martin Luther King. Often people want to attribute the power of the energy field to the leader because of his powerful way of speaking, which was particularly true of Dr. King. However, my belief is that it is the billions of thoughts of peace that come from the people, the followers of Martin Luther King, that generate the perceptible energy field that was found at the rallies where he spoke. He inspired the people, and contributed to the energy field, but it was the collective power of large numbers of people that was the basis of the civil rights movement. As a small child, I attended a march in Washington DC during the 1960's where Dr. King spoke, and I remember the heightened level of energy in the crowd of people.

Conversely, as is often the case, an energy field forms from a large number of base thoughts from a lower level of human existence; for example, thoughts of racism. Racism has been proven to be a false notion that was fabricated over 200 years ago to endorse the economic system of slavery. Yet, racist thoughts continue to linger in the Universal energy field in a rather strong form because those thoughts are *still* being projected into the world, even today. After so many years, how do these energy fields remain in place? Going back to the pond example; if someone is continuing to throw pebbles into the pond in a certain way, then the pond will always have a pattern of ripples that reflect the nature of those pebbles.

In the case of thoughts, the field of energy that is formed from the continuous tossing of racist thought pebbles into the Universal energy pond will result in the persistence of the racist field. Thankfully, the field of racism is diminishing in our lifetime, and I use it here as an example because it was a very powerful energy field in our society, but one that is perceptively shrinking as a result of our recent methods of collectively eliminating false beliefs from our reality.

The Law of Attraction states that energy is always attracted to energy of like kind. Therefore, your thoughts are always attracting other thoughts that are of a similar vibration. This is an extremely helpful concept to embrace in our personal lives. Thoughts of love attract more thoughts of love and the energy of Love into its field, and it compounds. So, one little thought of love attracts another, which makes two. The two thoughts together attract a few more, then several more, and then many more, until the thought energy field becomes strong enough to be recognized as a physical reality. This way of seeing the Law of Attraction at work is easy to acknowledge once people become tuned into subtle energy and watching for signs of it in action. For instance, synchronicity or serendipity is a daily occurrence for a growing number of people, especially for the ones who are watching for it. Synchronicity is the result of the interference pattern of thought waves that are there in the universe being noticed by someone. The wave patterns are already out there in the Source field, the synchronicity happens because we actually take notice of it, and bring that synchronistic event into our personal experience.

Another way of viewing thoughts in the Universal energy field is the model of the holographic universe as described by Talbot in *The Holographic Universe*. Images in holographic form are light waves that collide, and create "interference", that result in three-dimensional images. Thoughts behave the same way in the Universal field. Each thought that we have created individually, and collectively, exists out there in the universe as waves that operate at different frequencies, and interact with other waves to form complex interference patterns, that become what we call the real world. Therefore, the content of our thoughts is very important as they are cast into the Universe. Our minds are constantly racing with thoughts, and projecting them, somewhat randomly, into the universe. If we use intention with our thoughts, we can focus them, and not lose them to randomness. Focus thoughts on the universal goals of life that exist in infinite supply in the Universe such as love, peace, good health, friendship, close family ties, good community relations, connections to nature, fun, humor, and sex (why not?).

When you are thinking about practical matters and physical things, create thoughts of material abundance for what you need for your personal happiness in this lifetime. Having too much stuff is a serious problem for many people, particularly in the United States. Hoarding is a pathology that is unhealthy for humans. Create materially only what you really need, and evaluate that carefully. And consider renewable aspects of our present reality such as solar energy, food that can grown year after year, wood from forests that will regenerate, natural fibers, such as cotton and wool, that are continuously being re-grown on our planet. Even though recycling has become an established habit in most industrial societies, it's worth keeping in mind when buying products constructed of recycled and recyclable materials like steel, which can be used over and over, to create the abundance that we want to experience.

Additionally, include the well being of others in your thoughts so that all humans can benefit from your creative thinking. This strengthens the connection to all people and to the universal energy field, and ultimately strengthens the creation process, as we discover that we are all One. Envision healthy people living on a healthy planet. The Universe delivers for us the exact reflection of what we, ourselves, have put out into the Field. So, choose your thoughts with prudence.

Thoughts can be consciously conjured and delivered into the field in a variety of ways such as: reinforcement, emotions, gratitude, etc. that will be discussed further on. There are as many methods of generating thoughts as there are people on the planet, but here are some ideas for how to assemble thoughts for living Simply Abundant:

- Focus thoughts on the universal goals of life that exist in infinite supply in the universe.
- Create thoughts of material abundance for only what you need for happiness and consider renewable and sustainable aspects of creation.
- Keep in mind that thoughts are energy and they carry strength.
- Include the well being of other people in your thoughts.
- Place your thoughts in the context of all Creation.

Reinforcement

Thoughts that are cast into the Universal energy field are often somewhat lost out there in the infinite vastness of the universe. Like the seeds of a plant, thoughts are powerful little energy packets of potential, but they need tending. The analogy of the seed is excellent because the similarity between seeds and thoughts is quite profound. Seeds have the potential for the creation of a great plant or tree encapsulated in a tiny package that can sit dormant for long periods of time. Thoughts too, are little packets that contain tremendous potential. For realization of their potential, seeds need soil, water, sun, and certain methods of care. Thoughts need reinforcement from you, their creator.

Humans have at our fingertips several excellent tools for reinforcing the thought energy that we send out onto the Universal plane. Reinforcing thoughts is a highly personal process and each method should be used only to the extent that it feels authentic for you. The following are some good examples of reinforcement worth trying:

- **Writing** is perhaps the easiest way to reinforce thoughts that you have cast into the Universe. Writing, for me, is a powerful way to give meaning and strength to the thoughts I have put forth mentally. We know that thoughts are real at an intellectual level. By writing, thoughts become "real", as they physically appear on paper, or the computer screen, thereby giving them extra strength. Writing is a way of processing thoughts, and allowing them to flow through you. Julia Cameron describes this process well in her book *The Artist's Way*. Cameron advocates that people write three pages of handwritten thoughts each day which essentially serves as therapy for us. Personally, I start most days with writing, including intentions for the day, reflections on yesterday, inspirations, empowering thoughts, thanksgiving, dream documentation, etc. I have chosen a comfortable place on my couch in my living room, my favorite type of notebook, and a beautiful fountain pen, for my morning writing. All of this helps me develop good energy around my thoughts and writing.

- **Image Boards**: Some people are able to translate their thoughts artistically into images that can be drawn, painted or photographed into physical reality. Images can be cut from magazines or your own photos and put into a collage to reinforce your thoughts and visions. These vision boards are an easily accessible format and are fun and playful; they bring immediate good energy into your field, as you are constructing the vision board itself, and every time you view it in your home or office. Vision boards are your own creation, and should reflect your best and most abundant thoughts.

- **Affirmations:** Spoken reinforcement is another powerful tool that is preferred by many because it is so easy - just *say* it. If your intention for the day is to feel happy, and healthy, you can just say: "I am feeling happy and healthy today" upon waking up, in the shower, at breakfast, wherever; several times during the day is, in fact, preferable. Sound waves cast into the universe, like the thoughts themselves, are waves that exist eternally on the Universal plane.

- **Mantras** can be spoken, or chanted, and become quite powerful with repetition. Even a simple mantra that is personal to you is a way of reconnecting to your inner self and Spirit. You can repeat to yourself, at times throughout the day, a simple few words like: "I am Joy". Some of the most powerful vibrational experiences I have had in my life have been in a group setting where a mantra is being repeated. The power of many people's voices toning in resonance produces a strong vibration of sound waves that create harmony, both in a musical sense, and in a spiritual sense. This has been experienced by most that have done a simple Om mantra with a group. Also, if the harmonic sound is combined with the people's thoughts of the Divine being held by the group, the power is multiplied exponentially.

- **Singing** is another method for reinforcing thoughts that have been used for millennia, by people of many different cultures. Before written languages, oral histories were the preferred method of remembering things. Songs can serve the purpose of helping us to remember something, and the pleasant way that songs can be conveyed onto the Universal field, gives the thoughts extra strength. Songs can be repeated by others, and their force multiplied, as experienced by nearly everyone who has had song lyrics bouncing around in their heads for days on end.

- **Dance** is another technique used by the ancients to convey information. Inspired dancers in our culture could dance a thought into the Universal plane. Ecstatic dance is a transformational tool that can bring one to a higher state of consciousness, as the mind is sidetracked by the body's movements. Native American dance has always served tribes and communities as a method of accessing, or conveying, spiritual teachings. Sufi dance, Sama is ecstatic dance on the highest level of consciousness, and is a form of transformative meditation from the Sufi tradition within Islam.

- **Video:** For the technically advanced among us, there is a method for reinforcing thoughts using computer technology where you can create a personal inspirational movie to reinforce your thoughts. These multi-media videos are a composite of pictures, videos, music, written, and spoken messages that you can create yourself about *yourself.* Like a vision board, this vision video can be custom designed to reflect your own personal visions for your life.

Words are very powerful and transformative. Certain words trigger emotional responses in us that can be positive, or negative, depending on our relationship with the specific word. For instance, you can choose a more empowering word to describe the feeling of fear, by calling it *uncomfortable*, rather than *petrifying.* You can choose words that give you an uplifting feeling like, *stimulated*, instead of *stressed out.* Choosing words that are empowering gives you choice in the matter and allows you to be in the driver's seat of how you feel. Try it with any aspect of your life. Try changing the word for a food that you don't like from: "I hate that taste" to something more neutral like: "I'm not accustomed to that flavor". Words have been known to help people recover from illnesses, or plunge them deeper into sickness, depending on the actual word, and the person's experience with that word. Be careful, though not to choose words that have some residual impact from your past, or that have leftover emotional baggage from your childhood. For example, the word *strive* might have a positive impact for one person but possibly a negative impression for a young man whose mother said to him as a child: "you just have to strive harder", even though he may be trying his best. Transform the words you tell yourself to serve your higher self.

Each day, you can reinforce your intention and thoughts, using words that give the most positive impression, instead of words that are characteristic of failure. Use the empowering words in your daily writing, affirmations, poetry, songs, movies, or other reinforcement methods. I use a technique that I call *mind-chanting* to imprint ideas in my mind, and cast the thoughts into the field on a regular basis. One mind chant that I use is based on cheerleading. It is like you have a little cheerleading squad in your mind that gives you a boost, just like the cheerleaders give the football team some vibrational energy to keep going. Mind-chanting can be just between you and your personal cheering section, and you can say whatever you want to yourself, but make the chants a form of reinforcement of that which you want to create.

Creative visualization is one of the cornerstones of creating abundance consciousness. Images provide the creative process with the fuel that is needed for manifestation. Remember that the universe is overflowing with the raw material for creating reality, and your brain is the computer processor for making that happen.

In a technical sense, your eyes don't really "see" anything. When an object is placed in your field of vision, your eyes take in the information in the form of light through the eyes' lenses in a manner similar to a camera. The visual information is conveyed to the brain through the optic nerve and your brain processes that information and creates an image in your mind of what the object is supposed to look like. The image that the brain creates resides in the mind and we call it "reality". The eyes and the mind aren't "seeing" the object in the way we would like to believe. Instead, the eyes are taking in information, and the brain is interpreting that information, quickly creating visual images in our mind in a way that makes us believe we are seeing something as it actually is. The mind can be easily tricked in ways as demonstrated by the Old Lady/Young Women picture, where an image can be interpreted by the brain as being either an old lady with a shawl, or a young woman with a hat, depending on how you "see" the picture. Of course the image can be either an old, or a young woman; in fact, the image is both.

A stereogram will do the same thing with your brain when you stare at them long enough. The first image that the mind creates when the colorful information comes into the brain is a collage of color blotches. Then after staring at the center of the picture, or slightly off center to trick the mind that wants to just "see" the color blotches, the mind slowly relaxes. Eventually the image changes and new information that was underneath, or embedded in the colorful blotches comes into focus. This is a firsthand experience of the work of the brain to create two different images based on basically, the same information coming through the lens of the eyes. The colorful patterns of a stereogram are interpreted first one way to create an image, and then moments later, interpreted another way. The images in our minds are an *interpretation* of what is out in the world. We could see something one way, or see it a different way.

The images that our mind creates are what become our perception of physical reality. These images created in the brain are based on information taken in from the senses (sight, smell, sound, taste, touch). This is not the actual nature of the universe, as we have learned in the previous chapters of this book, but instead it is an interpretation of the vibrational information that the eyes have taken in, the brain has disseminated, and decided has form. The real nature of the universe is that an infinite number of possibilities exist in the energy field of reality, and we choose the one we want. Like a stereogram with embedded information that the mind needs a moment to sort out, the universe has embedded information that the brain hasn't quite figured out, yet. If the mind were to create a picture of what the universe really "looks" like, we might be blinded by infinite light, or we would be panic-stricken because there would be no actual "ground" to stand on, just interference waves of light. The world would basically be unrecognizable to us; we wouldn't understand what it was. One day, when human minds have an understanding of what the real nature of the universe is, we can comprehend it, and the mind will give us images that we can cope with. Those images though, may look nothing like what we now perceive the real world to look like.

When you close your eyes and create images in your mind, you are doing the same thing with your mind that you do when you are "seeing" something or "hearing" something: you are creating mental images based on information that the brain is processing. Therefore, when you create a picture of something in your brain during the visualization process, it is no less real than the picture that your brain creates when it gets information from your eyes - both are pictures created in the brain from vibrational information, and both exist in the field of Universal energy. The physical objects that you "see" with your eyes exist in the present reality that you have accepted as being real. The images that you create in your mind during a visualization process also exist in the energy field, but have not been brought into your present reality yet. Like when you view a stereogram, your mind takes in a certain amount of information and makes a decision about what it is. Your brain can sort out additional information, which then changes your mind's picture, and shifts your perception of your current reality – you can just "change your mind". Our perception of this so-called "reality" is a constantly changing process of reinterpreting information that the brain takes in. All the information is out there in the Field, it is just a matter of choosing which information you will call "real". Bringing things into your present reality is the process of manifestation that is the result of the all of the steps to Simple Abundance: Intention, Thoughts, Reinforcement, Emotions, Expectation, Gratitude, and Action.

Reinforcement is an important step in the creation process because, to the mind, one type of information is as crucial as any other form. Therefore, the images that you create in your mind with the visualization process are as real as anything else, and just as powerful. Visualization will help to bring into your present reality what you want to manifest by giving the brain new information. Your spirit already knows this. Your spirit/soul/ higher self knows the nature of the universe, and knows that the other realities are out there in full form, in the Universal field. Your brain probably knows that too. However, the brain needs a little help remembering; that's where visualizations come in. You are helping your own brain "see" the true nature of the universe. By giving the brain information in the form of pictures about your desired intention, you are helping the brain dial into the frequency of the Universal energy field where all possible futures already exist. That's why dreams are important – they are images from an alternate reality that we don't normally experience in daily waking life. But the dream world is real, and the spirit goes there every night, and brings back pictures, and film clips to share. Unfortunately, our brain doesn't know exactly what to do with these images, and we often dismiss them as being "unreal".

Remember that every possible alternative outcome already exists in the Universal energy field. The mind needs to be reminded of that, and you must create images to reflect that understanding. The visualization process is like shopping for images in a store that has every possible image "imaginable"; you can pull this or that picture off the rack, and see if it fits your intention. Remember to use images that are empowering to you, but also empowering for others. Use images that reinforce light, love and life, which are the natural elements of the universe. Select images from the infinite source of everything; those images that reflect your intention for yourself, your family, community, and the world. Close your eyes and create any image imaginable.

It's all a matter of choosing the reality that you want to create, and bringing that into your present reality. See Shakti Gawain's book, *Creative Visualization* for great tips on visualizing your goals and visions in life.

Emotions

Feelings are the key to happiness. OK, that says it all and it's true. So where do feelings of happiness come from? On the base level, your thoughts create your feelings, and the feelings come from your mind having analyzed all of the thought information in any moment in your life. In a process that is similar to the mind's interpretation of visual images, or other sensory information, the mind sorts all of the thoughts that are generated and decides what that combination of thoughts means to each of us. The ego weighs in on the decision process with its own interpretation, with a wide range of fears, based on past imprinted information. The brain then sends messages to the body that reinforce the feeling that the brain and ego have decided on. The body creates biochemical, and bioelectrical, signals that result in sensations that you experience as happiness, sadness, joy, disappointment, nervousness, elation, etc. The skin gets tingly, muscles get tense or relaxed, breathing is affected; the body's glands play a role, hormones flow, endorphins kick in, your stomach acids flow; your entire body responds to the idea that you are in an emotional state.

Unfortunately, at times the whole process is off track, based on flawed information that the mind is getting about what feeling is desired. If the mind thinks that the information coming from the ego is really important, or that a past experience should dictate the current emotion, then that is the direction that the mind goes. The mind does not remember that every possible emotion is available from the Universal field of all possibilities, and thinks that the options are limited, or that there is only one option available. Therein lies the pattern that our minds too often put into play: that there is only one option, which inevitably gives us a trapped feeling, with no way out. Feelings themselves come from the universal plane of consciousness where everything exists. Every feeling of happiness, or unhappiness, exists in the universe, and every moment you have the opportunity to select the feelings that support your intention; it is all a matter of choice.

Feelings are the key to unlock the door to manifestation which, at times, seems locked. You may have tried various other techniques to get what you want in life and then proclaimed that it "just didn't work". Remember that the outcome of your intention already exists in the Universal field where all outcomes exist. This is not a matter of "it" working, or not; both "working", and "not working", exist in the Universe. Our ability to select the "working" result takes effort because the concept that everything already exists in the universe does not fit our culturally supported worldview where there is only one possibility. That is why you need to support the visualization process by generating the emotions that are indicative of your intention.

If your intention is happiness in life, generate feelings of happiness that will give your mind extra information that can counter the ego, which may be sending a different message. Life coaches, and inspirational speakers, have been discussing the power of positive thinking for decades; they said: "you are what you think". The same can be said of feelings: you feel what you're feeling. You don't have to deny that you may, at times, be feeling negativity, sadness or the like. Just recognize that a different feeling already exists in the Universe and it is there, waiting for you. Negative feelings actually help you to see what you *don't want* feels like. You benefit from understanding that it is the contrast of this feeling, or another feeling, that helps you refocus on what you really want to experience. All possible feelings exist that range from really fantastically-high-flying great feelings to belly-scraping-in-the-mud low down feelings. All possibilities already exist, and can be chosen from the field to feed the interpretive process in the brain, in support of your intentions and visions of life.

Once again, with your eyes closed, imagine the feeling of happiness that you are intending to manifest, and create that feeling in your mind. Re-experience a feeling of happiness that you had in the past (that old feeling still exists in the Universal field, and is available for re-experiencing). Get into the details of that feeling and experience it at the body level. How does that feeling of happiness feel in your gut, your chest, your arms and legs? Are your muscles more relaxed? Does your heart soar with a memory of past happiness in life? Does it feel so good that you are actually physically excited, and want to get up and do something? Well, go ahead, get up, and do it, because that will help to strengthen the message that your brain is getting and sending back out into the universe. Then, remember what all of those good feelings are like so that you can recognize them again, and evoke them easily.

Expectation

Expectation might be a loaded word for some but I intend to clarify that a little in this section. I'm working my way around the word *hope*, which is an often used, but counterproductive word in our language. Since the universe is an infinite place of creation, it provides us with whatever our intention is. As the Law of Attraction always does, it delivers energy that is like-kind to that being generated. The emotion of hope will deliver exactly that: more hope. For instance the hope for peace gives people *hope*, not peace itself. If people put their thoughts toward peace itself it would go farther to bringing about peace on Earth. As active creators of our own reality, we don't need to "hope" for anything to happen, because we *know* that it will happen.

Expectation is altogether different from hope – it is a *knowing*. When you cast a thought into the flow of Universal energy, you should not be *hoping* for that in your life, you should be *expecting* that. You can have a different perspective that recognizes that what you have in mind already exists in the universe, and is now entering into your reality. After casting a thought into the Universal field, reinforcing it, and feeling it, close your eyes, and experience your intention as already existing, and coming into your life, with absolute certainty. There should be a deep feeling inside you that has no doubt that this vision of yours is in the process of manifesting and is very real. Practice this as often as possible to establish the neuro pathways that will convince your brain that it is the truth; this *is* happening.

Your brain sends messages to your body using a tremendously complex system of bio-chemical signals that are communicated across the brain in the form of neurotransmitters, which send signals across the brainwaves. In the biochemistry of your brain, there is a network of little switch-like connections called synapses. These synapse networks are like pathways carrying messages back and forth in the brain. These pathways are time-tested routes for certain messages that recur over and over in your life, and messages can be sent extremely quickly, using these familiar routes. Unfortunately, the brain gets accustomed to certain established pathways for sending signals and often chooses the "old" path, even though a different message is being sent. For that reason, creating new neuron pathways is critical to getting the brain to follow a different set of instructions. You need to have a deep conviction that the end result that you desire already exists in the universe, and is available to you; learn to expect the desired result. Messages of doubt carry their own energy, and encourage the brain to follow old routes carrying information that does not support your vision. Doubts promote thoughts of failure and feelings of despair, which cascade into a spiral that is damaging to the efforts of manifesting your vision.

Having an honest and heartfelt expectation that your intended vision already exists in the Universal plane of consciousness is critical for success. Expectation is powerful because it creates the new neuron pathways that your brain uses to send messages to your body, and out into the Universal field, to strengthen your vision. The energy state of your vision already exists in the Universe, and is in the process of coming into your reality. Every aspect of the manifestation process strengthens the energy of your intention, and brings it closer to coming into physical reality. Believe that it is so and it will be. We've probably all had many little experiences where good things that we'd wanted just sort of dropped in our laps; I'll share just one of mine. One day, my daughter and I were walking past the stadium where our town's women's basketball team plays. Outside, there was a hot dog vendor cart outside and a guy hawking dogs to the sports fans. My daughter loves hot dogs so we stopped for a couple of deluxe wieners and sat down outside the stadium to people-watch, as the fans filed in to watch the game. My daughter is a bit of a sports fan, so I thought it would be good to show her a game in which women excelled at a professional level, and I asked her if she ever thought about going to a women's basketball game. She said: "yeah, maybe someday it would be fun". About two minutes later, I spotted a friend of mine, who I waved to, and shook hands with as he walked up. He immediately offered me two tickets to the game that he couldn't use, and my daughter and I said OK; I guess this is the "someday" that she just mentioned.

Have the expectation that your intended vision exists in the Universe, and it is in the process of coming into your present reality now, tomorrow, or any other day. Believe that in your heart, but give no time table for manifestation because, after all, time doesn't exist anyway. Time is concept made up by people for a variety of reasons, and should not be part of our manifestation process, as we hold the expectation of our visions. So, during this stage of the manifestation process, give no thoughts to the little numbers on a watch, or on a calendar. Instead, have faith that the universe is a timeless container for everything that exists, ever did exist, or ever will exist. Have the expectation that your vision is in the process of manifestation in this moment, and know that the creative process is continuously at work manifesting from the energy that we put into it.

Gratitude

It's important to offer gratitude at this point in the process, because it acknowledges that the thoughts, emotions, and expectations that we have cast into the Universal field of energy, already exist in perfection. Everything that we can imagine already exists in the grand creation of the Universe; therefore, it's time to give thanks for whatever helped along the way. Gratitude and thanks are similar and I may use the terms interchangeably but they have a difference: the word gratitude carries with it a magnitude that surpasses the word "thanks' (which is what you tell the person at the cash register at the store when he gives your change). The word "thanks" has even been used sarcastically, which diminishes its manifestation qualities.

Gratitude is powerful because it also acknowledges the expectation that you are experiencing. Through expectation, you are imprinting the mind with thoughts that you are fully expecting the result of your intention, and since the Universal creative force is already at work, you are expecting manifestation, so gratitude is in order. Teachers, friends, and family members can be thanked at this time for their part. Giving gratitude to yourself is powerful because you deserve credit too. Serendipity (another byproduct of a creative Universe) can be thanked for happening at strategic moments. The abundant and prosperous planet Earth can be thanked. I often show gratitude to the Universe itself, for the immense creative miracle that it is. It is by the grace of this amazing abundant Universal energy that we are here on Earth having this experience at all.

Prayer is a technique that has been used for thousands of years by a diverse range of cultures. The conscious use of prayer is an excellent way to put your thoughts, or thanks, into the field. There have been hundreds of books written about how prayer can be used for positive good in our world (Marianne Williamson's *Illuminata, A Return to Prayer,* is a good one) so I won't expand much here.

Prayers are very personal connections with Source/God, and can have tremendous importance for us. If your prayers are delivered with true feelings, and your intentions are pure, these thought/ prayers will have a powerful influence in the Source field.

Once again, feel deep gratitude inside yourself for the people, or circumstances, that you are thanking. Just like thoughts are strengthened by genuine feelings, your gratitude can be strengthened by emotionally feeling deeply the love that comes from gratitude.

Actions

One part of the creative process that is often misunderstood is *action*, which is also critical for manifestation. In our culture there is too much emphasis placed on doing: oh come on, do something! do anything! just do it! Americans often believe that the only road to success is by *doing*, and we have Horatio Alger stories to give as an example of how it works. The overarching cultural story in the United States, and elsewhere, is that we are alone in the world and the only route to success is by individual action. This assumption is false, and often leads people to expend a large amount of energy in directions that are counter to their true intentions. At this point of the manifestation process, it is extremely important to keep your intention clear in your focus. Do not allow yourself to exert too much energy by means of action without checking in with your intention, and don't panic about timing (remember, time doesn't exist). This phase can be the most challenging but, this is where a lot of fun can happen.

The universe presents us with an infinite number of choices for action every instant and we wonder what actions will help us realize our intention. If I change jobs now, will that change my life? If I make the wrong move, will it ruin my chances for success at something else? In the context of Simple Abundance, action is the last part of the equation after we have set so much else in motion already. We have set an **intention**, offered our **thoughts**, **reinforced** our efforts, felt it **emotionally**, been in **expectation**, given **gratitude**, and now we are putting forth an **action** in support of our intention. This is the final step after significant amounts of vibrations have been applied to the Universal field. The Law of Attraction tells us that the action is much less important than the preliminary vibrational work. Sometimes, the only action to take is minimal, like buying the lottery ticket that reveals the winning numbers (one has to actually buy the ticket; you can't sit there and think of winning the lottery, and then not bother to buy the ticket). One of the ongoing limitations of living in a three-dimensional universe is that some action is required to make things happen.

When is the time for action? Sometimes we are throwing our actions into the energy mix way too early, before we have done our vibrational work. Ideally, we could put our intentions, thoughts, and gratitude into the Universal Source field right up to the moment that the action is called for. This is easier said than done. For instance, if you put out a desire into the field for something physical like a piece of furniture, there is a temptation to run out and buy it immediately. With a credit card, that's entirely possible, and sometimes, that's the answer. But if you can be patient long enough for the vibrations of your desire to line up in the energy field where all things exist, you might discover that the thing shows up in a most propitious way. There is no right or wrong way to act on a desire in life, even if you think that you blew your chance for a certain outcome. One thing to keep in mind is that the Universe will keep bringing your desire into your energy field, time and time again, to give you repeated chances to align with that which you desire, and with your current level of vibration. This is especially true with people who come into our lives. The right people always show up at the exact right time to show us something about our life's journey. Romantic partners show up, business partners arrive, friends come into our lives – all in the beautiful fashion that matches the vibrations that we are giving out.

The type of action required in your life is entirely a personal matter, and depends on where you are in your journey. Some of the big action items in our world today include: relationships, career decisions, making more money, locations for living, buying a house, investing, health and welfare choices, exercise, whether to start a family, retirement, travel plans, developing new interests, or making big purchases. In most cases, the first two, or three, action items occupy most people's minds, and tend to tie up our ability to co-create effectively. Most of our connections with nature, and other dimensions, are lost when we focus on the big life decisions like relationships, and career. Life is much more of a continuous series of little bite-sized decisions and actions, than it is a product of making huge, life-changing choices. Based on your **intention** being set in advance, you've created your **thoughts, reinforced** them, and experienced **emotions** that show you where you're at, you're **expecting** the result, so you show **gratitude**. Then, the slightest **action** effort brings it into your current reality.

What would happen if we flowed through life a little more gracefully and in balance with Mother Earth? What if we did most of our work vibrationally along the way, before taking action? What would it be like to take steps in life toward your intentions knowing that the vibrational preparation had been done? I propose that there are numerous little baby steps, and choices, throughout one's day, that give us the opportunity to gracefully be creators of our own reality, all of the time. That is the work of the next chapter, so please read on.

CHAPTER 9

Living Simply Abundant

"All that we are is the result of what we have thought"
The Buddha

Some of us find ourselves with one foot firmly on the ground, here in the three-dimensional world, and the other foot boldly in another realm, that I've been calling the Universal energy field, or Source. I have felt deeply connected to Mother Earth all of my life, and feel kinship with many animals, plants, and trees – what is commonly known as the "real world". I've also spent all of my adult life exploring different spiritual paths, and I am constantly discovering new wonders about Universal Source energy, and my co-creative role in the unfolding of reality.

How does one reconcile these different dimensional perspectives that are best described as the *physical world* and the *non-physical world*? How can we combine our love for Mother Earth, and acknowledge that the Law of Attraction is fully operational, in our lives, and in the universe in general? As I've said, I've been working on this for quite awhile, and I know that some things work for me, and other things don't. So what follows are some processes that have worked for me, as I've sorted out my life in multiple worlds, and concluded that these ideas are what allow me to live Simply Abundant.

So, let's see how being Simply Abundant in a normal day works, concerning one aspect of daily life. How can we use the knowledge and the techniques from the previous chapters to effect change in the Universal energy field in a positive way, in both our lives, and in the life of planet Earth? How about if we start with a reasonable intention, such as: *improving the nutritional quality of your food?*

Let's say you hold the basic value that food which is grown for consumption should be good for us, and should be grown in harmony with nature. It is a pretty general idea, but realistic enough that it is easy to imagine that we could hold that **intention**.

OK, so the intention is set, and our daily **thoughts** are oriented to healthy food with vitamins and minerals, that are needed by our bodies. Our thoughts also go out to the plants and animals which are contributing to our diet, and to the soil and water that has to support all of our lives, and to the larger ecosystem. We can be general in our thoughts, if that is easier – like holding the thought of a pastoral setting of a healthy farm in the countryside. We can be specific, and think of one of our favorite foods, such as apples, growing robustly in the sun on a healthy tree. Hold that thought!

We **reinforce** our intention by writing in our journals about the importance of nutrients to our body and our commitment to a wholesome diet. We talk to our friends and family about the quality of the food that they eat, where they shop, local farms, harvests, and other new information about food quality. We visualize the general good health of our bodies, and the health of the Earth, in meditation, or in quiet moments alone with ourselves. We can elaborate on our images as much as we want, and see ourselves living in optimum energy, and the planet thriving, as a Garden of Eden. We can connect with the plants and animals that we love. We can ask for the cooperation, or assistance, of the elemental spirits of specific minerals that may be important to us like, iron, calcium, or magnesium, and direct loving and positive energy to those minerals specifically. Use meditation or prayer or whatever works for you.

As we expand our intention, and our visions of improving the nutritional value of our food, we feel the **emotions** of satisfaction of knowing that our bodies are getting what they need. Our bodies return the energy with sensations that feel cleaner, healthier, and vibrant. Deep down, we feel that this is right, and our emotions tell us that we are on the right track, because we feel really good when we think about healthy food, and a healthy planet.

When we are in anticipation of improving the nutritional value of our food, we know that it is coming forward into our lives with each moment, and we **expect** that the nutritional uptake into our bodies is on the rise. We know that the Earth is better off, since we set our intention to improve our own food quality, and the conditions in which the food is grown. We expect health in our lives.

With the knowledge that the quality, and nutritional value of our food is improving, we can show **gratitude** for this profound change in our lives, and the planet. We may choose to give thanks quietly in prayer, or meditation, or as a passage in a notebook. If we are so inclined, we may want to perform a ritual of gratitude alone, or with others, as an act of thanksgiving. Native Americans sometimes will make an offering of tobacco (used in a sacred manner) back to the Earth in gratitude for her gifts to us. Or, you can give a silent statement of gratitude to the plants and animals that went into a meal, as you taste their delicious offering of flavor at dinner.

Throughout our day, we will find opportunities to put our intention into **action**. These opportunities will spring up like a fountain when our intention is strong, and Universal energy field has been seeded with powerful thoughts, reinforced, and visualized, felt and expected, and appreciated. Synchronicity, serendipity, and luck, will come our way on a regular basis, and one needs to be alert to these interference wave patterns in the field, as they are revealed to us. A healthier planet, and more nutritionally valuable food, will come into our experience.

There are many possible actions to take to improve the nutritional value of food. Let's take a detailed look at a somewhat routine task in life: a shopping trip to the grocery store, and see what potentialities exist at the store. This is a series of tasks with numerous possible outcomes, but that are enfolded into one action that we call *shopping*. Here is how someone living Simply Abundant could approach a grocery shopping trip:

- You've made a list of the healthy food that you really need and will be less tempted to buy junk food that calls to you from the shelf when you shop without a list.
- When you shop for food, try to do so when you are not terribly hungry; it limits the impulse buying which often results in regretted purchases.
- Set an intention that this shopping trip will be fun for you and the most beneficial for all of creation.
- Bring the bags that you'll need.

- Before heading out to the store, you will have decided that the method of transportation will be the least impactful as possible, so you might choose between walking with a bag, biking with a basket, the bus, sharing a ride with a friend, or driving by yourself. You might make your transportation choice on the size of your carefully prepared shopping list.

- When you get to the store you might hold the door for someone. That would feel good for you, and for the other person; they will probably say thank you kindly, and that will feel good too. Win – win, before you've even started the shopping!

- Chose a cart or basket that is the size appropriate for your shopping list, and mode of transportation.

- Shop first around the edges of the store where the essential whole food items usually are: vegetables, fruit, fish, meat, dairy, eggs, etc.

- When looking at the produce, you have to make the all-important organic or non-organic decision. Perhaps in some cases, locally produced, non-organic is more aligned with what you want to support. Maybe for certain things, organic is a must.

- Maybe you brought your own plastic produce bags to use, which are reusable many times over.

- Consider not using a bag at all for certain things such as: bananas, bundles of carrots, a single onion or squash.

- Balance price with the other factors. Sometimes, buying the cheapest doesn't deliver the value in terms of freshness, vitamins, etc.

- There might be certain foods on your list that give you a good feeling when you see them, like a variety of apples might be glowing in a certain way that tells you that the

Universe is responding to your energy of desiring better nutrition.

- Consider the meats and dairy foods carefully. The action of buying these foods will have a significant impact on your body's health, and on the health of the planet. Think about the way the animals were raised, or harvested. If you decide to purchase meat or fish, you may want to say a silent prayer of gratitude to the animals who gave their lives for our sustenance.
- If you are vegetarian or vegan, the outer edges of the store also carry items that you may be looking for.
- Pause here for a moment, and check your list. When you start down the long rows of packaged food items, it can be stressful. In these aisles there are going to be lots of things to look at that are just begging to be purchased (especially if you're hungry).
- The middle aisles of the store are also the location of some of the most heavily industrialized food items in the world. This is where it is helpful to read the labels to determine approximately what is in the cans, jars, and boxes that line the shelves. The vital life energy has left some of this food completely, and you will be able to sense this as you become more aware. The vibe in these aisles is definitely of a lower frequency, and you may also get a subtle message from the Universe to completely avoid certain aisles. Watch for someone with a giant shopping cart that is completely blocking the aisle – that's a sign to skip the aisle. If there is spilled food, or a puddle of gooey liquid on the floor – skip the aisle, this is the Universe giving you a heads up.
- You may want to make some of your decisions based on how much of the packaging can be recycled. Some

companies are doing a good job of this, but one still has to watch out for over-packaging. Double and triple-wrapping is wasteful even if it is recyclable.

- For practical reasons, the frozen section should probably be last. That's good because here is another domain of industrial food production. Think about alternatives to frozen food items which are somewhat removed from being actual food (frozen dinners for example). If the frozen food aisle feels, well, *freezing cold*, get the hell out of there!

- Consider leaving impulse purchases, and treats, to the end, if at all.

- At the checkout stand, I get a kick out of the tabloids, what can I say? As the Law of Attraction teaches, you can't know what you *do* want unless you know what you *don't* want.

- I also like conversing with the checkout people. They have a tough, somewhat monotonous job, and they always appreciate a complement, or cheerful attitude from customers. Who knows, he or she, might be working on their own process of intention, and what you say to them might be just the puzzle piece that they needed to manifest something in their life.

- You may want to keep a little something (maybe it's a coin, a dollar or a silent prayer) for the guy outside the door with his sign. If he is hungry, you could offer him one of the bananas that you just bought.

Wow, that sounds like a lot of action choices for a simple trip to the grocery store. But most of these are micro-choices that happen in a split second. The point is, that activities such as shopping, can be done with intention instead of as a dull habit. The reward of shopping with intention is having nutritious food for your body, but also having made purchases that are in alignment with your deeper relationship with the Earth. Be sharp about what the Universe is telling you as you move from home, to the store, and home again. Because of the dynamic nature of the Universe, there will be interactions between you, your surroundings, and the energy vibrations of the food itself. Also, there is the bonus of all of the opportunities for good interactions with fellow humans, shopping just like you, and who are looking to improve the nutritional quality of their food. When you offer good vibrations on the Universal field, people all around you will naturally pick up that vibe, and their lives will be uplifted.

As you go through your day, there will be hundreds of decision points where you can decide whether to create with intention, or to create unintentionally; either way, you are creating. I like to chose with intention, and make every choice a part of co-creating my reality in harmony with Mother Earth, and in vibrational concordance with Source. You might not be able to follow a process like we just did for improving the nutritional quality of food for everything in your life, but please do so for as many of your life intentions as possible.

Here are some other actions associated with living Simply Abundant that I do in my daily process of creation and you may consider in your life:

- I like to take short showers, knowing that the flow of abundant fresh water on Earth will last forever, if we take care of it.
- Whenever I get ready to leave home for any reason, I think about how I'm going to get where I'm going.

- I like walking because of the fresh air, and the chance to see the sky, and connect with trees and soil. So, I do as much as I can in my day by walking where I'm going.
- I take the bus places because I like to watch people, and exchange positive vibrations with my fellow bus riders. I've found that everyone who rides the bus is a teacher.
- Whenever possible, I eat whole, fresh vegetables, grains, and nuts, because I know they are plentiful, and that the Earth can provide them perpetually.
- I used to keep chickens for their beautiful brown eggs that they lay in abundance. I loved those girls, and they loved me back, by gifting me with eggs.
- Electricity is infinitely available, and I use only what I need, knowing that it will always be accessible to me in the future.
- I love to donate books, clothes and furniture to second hand stores, and then shop for other things to buy there. It feels prosperous to just give something away. And it feels prosperous to turn around and buy as much stuff as I want, use it for awhile, and then bring it back, and donate it again, knowing that someone else can use it for awhile. Some well made things can cycle on like that for years.
- The Sun seems to keep coming up in the east and setting in the west day after day. That beautiful sight is infinitely available, and I enjoy the magnificent view whenever possible.
- I love to draw, and paint, and my happiness is boundless. My potential pictures are limitless. I love to see other people's art, knowing that art is immortal and infinite.
- I appreciate music of all types, with the knowledge that the combination of musical notes and melodies offer endless variations of delight. Music is infinite.

- I choose laughter as often as I can in my day. There are no limits to the joy of a good laugh, and studies show that laughter can extend your life and health.
- I recycle paper because I know that the abundant forests will live forever, if we make paper from old paper, instead of cutting down trees; and I love trees.
- I donate money to organizations that are doing good work, like helping people to raise their vibrations, or organizations who are devoted to honoring nature.
- I protect spiders from harm. They eat mosquitoes, and I appreciate that.
- When I love, it is deeply, and with great enthusiasm.

I encourage you to make choices in your day with the intention of creating the life that you want in harmony with Earth, and in alignment with your Higher Self, and Source. A life of Simple Abundance will provide all that you need for experiencing the joy that everyone wants in life, which is our true purpose of being here on Earth at this time.

In abundance consciousness circles, it is often heard that someone wants to use the Law of Attraction to manifest a new car, maybe a Rolls Royce! That is a very common desire among Americans, and it's understandable in our auto-oriented society. But, I've always wondered, how would it be possible for everyone to own a Rolls Royce? There just aren't that many of them around. Besides, they get terrible gas mileage and they're hard to park. OK, well, what if you took the idea of car *ownership* out of the equation, and just let people manifest the Rolls for a night, or a week? I'll bet you that there are enough luxury cars and yachts in this world, and if everyone could be happy with a time-share arrangement...well then, we would all get to manifest some luxury now and then. Truthfully, whenever I've had the burning desire to own something non-essential, and then ran out and bought it, it's ended up in the closet, where it sits, unused. What I'm proposing is that all of that unused luxury stuff be pulled out of the metaphorical closet and made available to people to use on a part-time basis. Voilà, we have a planet full of happy people who can experience luxury items, and have the rich-feeling emotion that goes along with it. It is, after all, the feeling of richness that we are after. You can rent a villa in Italy without having to *own* it.

There are dozens of ways that people can share things in our world today; we don't all have to *own everything*. One can take advantage of the car sharing programs that are appearing in large cities in the US, making it possible to live in a city without actually owning an automobile at all. Most anything can be rented and you can experience the fun of having it for that duration of time, without being stuck with it in your closet. We are a society hung up on ownership, but we have alternatives. With all the incredible entrepreneurial minds working on new ideas, I'd say that there are an abundance of ideas out there for re-defining what it means to feel rich. Feelings of richness come from inside the mind, where all feelings are generated.

At some point, the day will come when human kind will develop our alchemical abilities more thoroughly. We will start to rearrange molecules with our thoughts, and a more direct form of physical creation will become part of our living experience. Anything is possible when we are co-creating our reality in alignment with the all-powerful energy that created our universe. I can imagine traveling forward or backward in time, moving between dimensions, or transporting ourselves across vast distances in space, when we leave this 3-D world of ours behind. Ultimately, the basis of our universe, and *ourselves*, is energy. Once we learn to vibrate in harmony with Source, all things are possible. If you think that creation, at any level, is a worthy cause, start with Simple Abundance, and enjoy the abundance of love, peace, and joy in your life. Start to build momentum with your creation work, and discover the other levels of abundance unfolding in our Universe. Work your way up the vibrational ladder, and you may be surprised at the amazing things that happen in your life. And, when many millions of people are creating the abundant universe together, just hang on; it might be an exciting ride.

CHAPTER 10

We Can Change the World

**"Imagine there's no countries, no religions too.
Imagine all the people, living life in peace"**
John Lennon

The previous chapter explained how individuals can have an effect on their personal reality by making choices, and targeting their thoughts in a certain way toward a desired outcome. We can create a new way of living gently on the Earth, by using the power of our thoughts to co-create that reality in the Source field, where all possibilities exist. If we do this in large numbers, we change the world toward an outcome that we all want: life on Earth that is peaceful, loving, and joyful, and honors all other life on this planet that we share.

As Jesus said to his followers: "For where two or three are gathered in my name, there I am in the midst of them". That passage, from Matthew 18:20 (Holy Bible, King James Version), can be interpreted different ways. I see it saying that positive energy fields can be created when even small numbers of people gather, and generate thoughts of love and peace, as Jesus would have advocated. Individually, we can accomplish changes to our own reality and, by osmosis to the larger culture. Together, we can put into effect a vibrational influence in the Source field that is exponential. Even in small gatherings of like-minded people, you'll find perceptible levels of positive energy that are commensurate with the vibrations that are being put out by those present.

Our joint thoughts, the *collective consciousness*, as Carl Jung called it, are creating the societal reality. We've seen it work for good, and we've seen it work for not-so-good. How can we direct these thoughts to create the world that we want to live in? People have used group prayer to reduce crime, with the result that violent crimes have declined in the United States, since the mid-1980s. The Maharishi Effect shows that when a specific number of people meditate together to effect a beneficial outcome, such as reduced crime, then the result is realized. Maharishi University research has shown that, if the number of meditators is equal to the square root of 1% of the population of a city, then noticeable changes in the vibration of that city, and the resultant behaviors of the population can be seen (see Maharishi University research at www.mum.edu). Worldwide terrorism has declined since hundreds of individuals, and groups around the world, have dedicated prayer and mediation sessions to peace on Earth. World wars and nuclear catastrophes have been narrowly avoided on numerous occasions in the past 50 years, by a force that we can attribute to the thoughts of those who hold the vision of peace.

Here, in the 21st Century, we stand poised at a grand decision point. On one side is the old destructive path we've been on; the other, is a new paradigm of wholeness and connection. By using co-creative methods together, we have an opportunity to steer our world away from our past fixation on separation, and instead toward Oneness. Using what we learned in the previous chapters about how to work individually with the interactive, vibrational Universe, we can also join our minds in co-creation with each other, and Source.

Many have spoken of the current time period, including Native American prophets, ancient texts, and modern theologians. Recently, David Korten in his book, *The Great Turning*, describes a vision of how a new world might look. Korten calls the paradigm shift that is in front of us The Great Turning (a term he borrowed from Joanna Macy), because this is an opportunity to turn away from 5,000 years of history spent on empire-building, toward world societies based on cooperation with each other, and nature.

Some voices are quick to say that people have always competed with each other, and that empires have been the human vehicle for advancing themselves. This was largely true for the past 5-10,000 years. But, as was pointed out earlier in Chapter 5, humans lived for thousands of years prior to the current empire-building period, in a variety of cooperative social structures. Tribal people living in cooperative societies give us numerous examples of how it can be accomplished. Humankind has much to look upon as reference material, for use in crafting a new society structure, based on cooperation and wholeness. There are some communities of people who have been living here in peace, side by side with empire-building, for all of the past 5-10 millennia. The great majority of peaceful societies have been annihilated by aggressive forces, but nonetheless, many still remain to this day, to serve as role models. Much of the Tibetan culture, which has peace as a national priority, is still intact, even after 50 years of occupation by Chinese forces. Aboriginal people of the

Australian continent have lived in close contact with the forces of Earth energy continuously for 30,000 years, and have kept that knowledge throughout the 200 years of occupation by people of European origin. Many indigenous tribes still thrive deep in the Amazon region of South America. In fact, small indigenous tribal cultures have survived on every continent, despite tremendous pressure from European colonialism, and other invasions.

We can take what civilization has given us, in terms of the wealth of knowledge and science. We can absorb the wisdom that the indigenous people have carried with them over millennia, and combine the wisdom and knowledge into a new system of understanding.

Many religious organizations have stayed close to their philosophical foundations, including the Friends (Quakers), who have never participated in any of the dozens of wars in countries where they have lived over the past 300 years. Individuals have made tremendous contributions to reinforcing the peaceful energy input into the Universal energy field. In my lifetime, Mother Teresa with her work in Calcutta, and Martin Luther King in the United States, have been powerful voices for peace. Mahatma Gandhi, living in the first half of the 20th Century, gave one of the best examples of being politically active, while also a peaceful agent of change. Nelson Mandela, more recently, in South Africa, was an exemplary person of peace and tolerance.

There have been numerous movements to create democratic, self-governed communities of people living cooperatively, here in the United States just in the past 100 years. Community-building efforts recently have included the intentional community movement of the 1960's and 70's, that continues today. Additionally, the development of cohousing communities throughout the United States, and many other countries in Europe, represents a strong effort for people of the modern world to rebuild the connected communities of the past. There are currently over 100 cohousing communities in the U.S. with many more in the planning phases. Cohousing communities consist of anywhere from a few families to 30 or 40 families, living in close proximity, sharing resources and meals, often growing their own food, making decisions jointly, consciously choosing to live life differently from the general direction of the dominant society. Despite the pressure our society is under to fragment, people's need to be connected through community continues today.

Humans in the 21st Century have many things to be hopeful about. Most encouraging of all, is the understanding that a new human society already exists in the Universal Source field, where everything already exists, energetically. A new human society, based on connected people, living in peaceful harmony with all beings, on our beautiful planet, already exists in the Source field, complete, and waiting for us; people just need to choose it. What I just described is difficult for some people to accept, because there is so much built up negativity. But when viewed as *remembering*, our connection to Source becomes easier to see. Humans now are remembering that we are on this planet to create beauty, and connect with the Universal flow of love. Source is here to support us, and create with us the experience of abundant love.

We don't necessarily need to completely understand the multi dimensional aspects of the universe to choose to live that way. By choosing to connect with Universal energy, people are bringing a new world of love and peace into our present reality. Each of the decisions we make, moment to moment, acts to bring into reality the paradigm shift toward wholeness, and away from separation. David Korten gives the example of the Monarch butterfly that starts life as a voracious caterpillar that consumes many times his weight in food. The caterpillar then attaches itself to a twig, and starts a metamorphosis that eventually changes all the cells in his body, and transforms the creature into a beautiful, flying, angel-like butterfly that devotes its life to living a gentle and beautiful existence on Earth, pollinating plants in a benevolent way. Such a transformation might be unimaginable to a lowly caterpillar, but deep in its soul, at a cellular level, it knows what it will become – the butterfly already exists vibrationally and is genetically imprinted in the caterpillar. We human beings can frame our transformation as such.

There is no doubt that we live on a planet that provides abundant splendor for all of the creatures who live here, and that is evidenced by the tremendous growth of the human species over these many years. Humans have developed, or always have had, the ability to change, or adapt to different conditions, with resultant prosperity. Humans live in the extremely cold conditions of the arctic, and deep in tropical rainforests, and they have prospered for their adaptations. As omnivores, we humans eat an incredible variety of foods: from large mammals to plants, and even fungus. In the process, we find a dizzying number of different ways to prepare this abundant banquet. We have found amazing uses for the world's mineral and biological resources, and created technologies that are changing our lives even further. Human beings, through our individual and collective consciousness, have created this setting that we live in.

Now, picture a world in which people live in harmony and peace with each other; where everyone understands that we are all connected in a matrix of energy on the Universal plane of consciousness. Imagine that wars and hatred become things of the past, just as the institution of slavery is a relic that our culture has abandoned. We can abandon other concepts that don't work for our world. Possibly, the borders of nations can be loosened, and the concept of "nationalism" itself can be tossed in the historical dust bin for the betterment of our future planet. We can look to John Lennon's words at the beginning of this chapter, and we can *imagine*. We shall imagine because imagination is powerful. Albert Einstein once said: "Imagination is more important than knowledge. For knowledge is limited to all we now know and understand, while imagination embraces the entire world, and all there ever will be to know and understand". Imagination is unlimited.

The new paradigm shift may create a world where each person feels like they are part of the human family, as well as part of a distinct ethnic group. People have always been joined together in ethnic groups where they share language, traditions, and lifestyles, which will continue, and flourish with new tolerance and joy in sharing ethnic variety. People will share the facets of their cultures and we will all be enriched. The human family is, of course, a subset of all of life on the planet, so people can say that they are part of a planetary family. This community of life on Earth shares DNA that tells the story of a family of beings that are all bound together at a genetic level. One could also consider themselves a citizen of the galaxy, connected to all of creation through the vibrations that hold the galaxy together. Ultimately, we can see ourselves as partners in the creation process, helping to create the beautiful reality of our universe.

This is the evolution of the human race. Human DNA may already be shifting, and making changes to accommodate the changing circumstances and forging the genetic makeup of a new human being. For centuries, scientists have been studying the phenomenon of organisms adapting to their environment by way of changes to their DNA make-up. Jean Lamarck, French scientist of the 18th Century (who preceded Darwin), suggested that living creatures <u>chose</u> to change themselves to adapt to different conditions. It stands to reason then, that humans will be able to change themselves in many ways, including at the genetic level, to become a new type of co-creative human being.

Some evidence of DNA changes is manifesting with the number of Indigo children who are being born into this age, with extraordinary psychic abilities. Indigo children, whose DNA is shifting to the new paradigm, will be giving birth to their own children someday, whose chromosomes will have some of the same DNA coding and will be passed to *their* offspring. We may, actually, be in the process of changing our DNA during the performance of Simple Abundance visualizations and manifesting. Each thought and emotional message sent into the Universal field carries with it the energy that can interact with subatomic particles, and DNA, as well. Many people have used visualization techniques to cure themselves of common ailments and debilitating diseases. This is the same process of sending thought energy, and emotional energy, into the Universal plane of consciousness to interact at the cellular level of the human body. Anything is possible.

During this paradigm shift, old animosities between nations will drop away easily, as we discover our connection on higher vibrational planes of consciousness. Differences between religions and cultures will have little importance compared with the greatness that can be accomplished by people when we are connected to each other, and all of creation. Differences will evaporate more quickly than can be imagined. We have witnessed this phenomenon in the relationship between the powers of World War II that united against the rest of the world - Germany, Italy, and Japan, and the forces that fought against them, including the United States. The United States sees these three countries as some of our closest friends now, and the feelings are reciprocated. How is it possible that the American military can drop two atomic bombs on heavily populated cities in Japan, creating holocaustic results and then, less than a generation later, the two countries are the closest of friends, connected culturally in myriad ways? I've met many people from Japan who show no signs of hatred, or festering ill feelings, toward Americans. On the contrary, they want to meet Americans, learn English, and listen to American music, etc. The example of the United States and Japan gives me great hope that the wounds of past horrors can be forgiven, and the human race can move on to the next level of evolution.

Simple Abundance is a particularly attractive world-wide vehicle of change because one doesn't have to leave home to participate. The internet provides the conduit to link people from around the world, and therefore, their combined energies are amplified as the concerted thoughts are cast into the Universal Source field. Already, the internet and social media has facilitated the downfall of several dictators in the Middle East, and North Africa, starting with President Ben Ali in Tunisia, which launched the "Arab Spring" in 2011. Action was carried out in the streets in Tunisia, Libya, and Egypt, but only after the vibrational field had been fully charged with thoughts of freedom, and democracy, and projected by millions of people in those countries. Vibrationally, the dictators were done before the Arab Spring began.

The new world that we are creating will be *very* connected, and not just through the internet. Imagine the power of the internet at the level of conscious connections! Imagine closing your eyes and connecting to people around the world at a heartfelt level of connection. The possibilities are limitless. When people learn to connect at these other levels, the flow of information can be shared instantly. I've already seen this happening among those of us who are vibrationally connected, and have experienced "intuitive hits" and synchronicities together.

How can environmentally and socially conscious people affect similar results on the other human institutions that are undesired? The social ills of aggression, injustice, war, poverty, and the resultant environmental degradation are still held in place by the thoughts and intentions of the past vibrational frequency (remember that the Law of Attraction delivers to us the reality that we have given attention to). Pollution, soil depletion, desertification, over-fishing, rainforest destruction, falling water tables, and such, can be considered the result of bad vibrations – bad vibes that humans have been putting out into the Universal field over time.

How can we replace the vibrations of destruction with a new world paradigm of love, peace and joy? By diligently following the process set forth in Chapter 8 on an on-going basis, changes in the vibrations will create changes in our world's reality. And with the full faith and belief that the values of our new way of living already exist in the Source field, they will manifest in our lives, and the lives of our fellow human beings. You can hold a higher vision for yourself, your family, your community, and all of humanity. Hold a vision for all of Creation and let the waves of love, peace, and joy radiate out to them through the Universal Source field.

Some possible ideas for spreading the vision further:

- Using social media is an obvious way to gather with others. Use **Facebook, Twitter,** or any other way of connecting with others.
- Gather a group in your home. Websites such as **Meetup,** enable you to easily start a group, or join an existing group, to co-create together.
- Join an already established on-line group that coordinates mass intention setting. The **GaiaField Project** and the **Intention Experiment** are two well established places to join in the global movement for vibrational change.
- Give financially to organizations doing this work; money is just another form of energy after all.
- Volunteer in person somewhere. Remember, though, that any action should follow the vibrational work that is so integral to living Simply Abundant.

Consistency, diligence and persistence are all important to maintaining your levels of energy. From your unlimited inner source of energy will come more and more power to put into thoughts of a new peaceful society that we are in the process of creating. The shifting of spiritual energy on Earth has been in the works for so many years now that the raising of vibrational levels is accelerating. Each one of us is part of an interconnected network of love energy in tune with Source, which is actively creating the abundance around us. Now is the time to add your beautiful vibrations to the world-wide frequency of love, peace, and joy.

R. Frank Robinson is a professional landscape architect and devoted spiritual seeker. He has spent his life studying nature and practicing environmental design while simultaneously searching the inner realms for an understanding of the nature of reality. Inspired as a youth by the design work of Frank Lloyd Wright, and then transformed by spiritual teachings, he has balanced his passion for physical nature and his love for non-physical Divine Source. Frank has lived in intentional communities, small towns, and large cities, and currently lives in Seattle, Washington.

Bibliography

A Course In Miracles. Mill Valley, CA: Foundation For Inner Peace, 1976

Bohm, David. *Wholeness and the Implicate Order.* Oxford, UK: Routledge Publishing, 1980

Brown, Lester. *Full House, Reassessing the Earth's Population Carrying Capacity.* New York, London: Worldwatch Institute/W W Norton, 1994

Cameron, Julia. *The Artist's Way, A Spiritual Path to Higher Creativity.* New York, NY: Jeremy P. Tarcher/Putnam, 1992

Capra, Fritjof. *The Tao of Physics.* Boston, MA: Shambhala Publications, 1975

Diamond, Jerod. *Collapse, How Societies Choose to Fail or Succeed.* New York, NY: Viking Press, 2005

Diamond, Jerod. *Guns, Germs, and Steel, The Fates of Human Societies.* New York, NY: WW Norton, 1997

GaiaField Project. www.gaiafield.net

Gawain, Shakti. *Creative Visualization.* Mill Valley, CA: Whatever Publishing, 1986

Gore, Al. *Our Choice, A Plan to Solve the Climate Crisis.* Emmaus, PA: Rodale, Inc., 2009

Greene, Brian R. *The Elegant Universe, Superstrings, Hidden Dimensions, and the Quest for the Ultimate Theory.* New York, NY: W.W. Norton, 1999

Hawking, Stephen W. *A Brief History of Time, From the Big Bang to Black Holes.* New York, Toronto, London, Sydney, Auckland: Bantam Books, 1988

Hawkins, David R. *Power vs. Force, The Hidden Determinants of Human Behavior.* Carlsbad, CA: Hay House, 1995

Hicks, Esther and Jerry. *Ask and It Is Given, Learning to Manifest Your Desires.* Carlsbad, CA: Hay House, 2004

Hill, Napoleon. *Think and Grow Rich.* Meriden, Connecticut: The Ralston Society, 1937

Kasser, Tim. *The High Price of Materialism*, Cambridge, MA: MIT Press, 2002

Kaku, Michio. *Parallel Worlds, A Journey Through Creation, Higher Dimensions, and the Future of the Cosmos.* New York, NY: Anchor Books, 2005

Korten, David. *The Great Turning, From Empire to Earth Community.* San Francisco, CA, Kumerian Press, Bloomfield, CT and Berrett-Koehler Publishers, Inc. 2006

Larkin, Amy. *Environmental Debt, The Hidden Costs of A Changing Global Economy.* New York, NY: Palgrave MacMillion, 2013

Macy, Joanna. www.joannamacy.net/

Maharishi University research. www.mum.edu

McTaggert, Lynn. *The Field, The Quest for the Secret Force of the Universe.* New York, NY: Harper Collins, 2002

McTaggert, Lynn. The Intention Experiment, www. theintentionexperiment.com

Murphy, Joseph. *The Power of the Subconscious Mind.* Lakemont, GA: CSA Press, 1975

Nadeau, Robert and Menas, Kafatos. *The Nonlocal Universe, The New Physics and Matters of the Mind*. Oxford, UK: Oxford University Press, 2001

Robin, Vicki and Dominguez, Joe. *Your Money or Your Life: 9 Steps to Transforming Your Relationship with Money and Achieving Financial Independence*. New York, NY: Penguin Group, 1992

Ruhela, S.P. and Robinson, Duane, ed. Sai *Baba and His Message, a Challenge to Behavioural Sciences*. Delhi, India: Vikas Publishing House, 1976

Sahlins, Marshall. *"The Original Affluent Society"* (abridged), ch.5, pp79-98. *The Politics of Egalitarianism: Theory and practice*, ed. Jacqueline Solway. NY: Berghahn Books, 2006

Stone, Merlin, *When God Was A Women*. New York, NY: Barnes and Noble, 1976

Talbot, Michael. *The Holographic Universe*. New York, NY: Harper Perennial, 1991

Union of Concerned Scientists. www.ucsusa.org

Wackernagel, Mathis and Rees, William. *Our Ecological Footprint, Reducing Human Impacts on the Earth*. Gabriola Island, BC, Canada: New Society Publishers, 1996

Weisman, Alan. *The World Without Us*. New York, NY: St. Martin's Press Thomas Dunne Books, 2007

Williamson, Marianne. *Illuminata, A Return to Prayer*. New York, NY: Random House, 1994

Williamson, Marianne, *A Return to Love, Reflections on the Principles of A Course In Miracles*. New York, NY: Harper Collins, 1992